"Lilyan Wilder helps the TV neophyte to become good, fast. Her aim isn't to make you different in front of a camera, but to help you project the person you really are."

Jane Bryant Quinn

"An extraordinarily gifted coach! Lilyan's advice can change your life and take you to a new level as a communicator."

John Sculley, Partner, Sculley Brothers, LLC

"With tips that will benefit everyone from the most timid beginner to the most seasoned professional, *7 Steps to Fearless Speaking* is a must for anyone who needs to speak in public."

Bill Baker, President, WNET-TV

"Lilyan Wilder is a pro who shares her insights and wisdom so that many can benefit. How lucky we are to have *7 Steps to Fearless Speaking*."

Elizabeth Rohatyn, former Chairman, New York Public Library

"Lilyan Wilder is simply the best. She makes you think about what you're saying, how you're saying it, and even why you're saying it. She's ethical, honorable, and wonderful."

Carol Marin, Correspondent, CBS News

"When I started in television, they said my voice was raspy. Now they say it is distinctive. Lilyan Wilder helped make the difference."

Dick Schaap, Author, Broadcaster

"There is no sweeter music, or more vivid picture than that formed by the human mind and voice. And there is no better teacher to help a person unleash the beauty and power of speech than Lilyan Wilder."

Garrick Utley, Correspondent, CNN

"Ms. Wilder's no-nonsense approach helps you find that big voice inside and overcome the trauma of public speaking."

Francine LeFrak, President, LeFrak Productions

P9-ELS-020

ACCOLADES AND AFFIRMATIONS FROM STUDENTS OF LILYAN WILDER

"I got a lot of experience and help in overcoming my fears about speaking in public. Lilyan Wilder has so many good ideas about how to change the focus away from the self-conscious self and towards the audience, where it belongs."

"I've learned to project, to engage, to get a response as soon as possible, and to have a definite structure—beginning, middle, and end."

"I think what helped me the most is the voice exercises. They help me control the shakiness that my voice sometimes gets when I get nervous."

"The most helpful ideas were the suggestions on how to be private and personal with your audience. Also, speech outlines were very helpful."

"Three months ago I would've worried about this for days and days and days. I wouldn't have done the preparation. Now I am able to take a reasonable amount of time and put together something that is coherent and not worry about it. Now that I realize that I am capable of doing that I'm not afraid of it."

"I felt like I had techniques that would help me get through this. It finally got to the point where being afraid just wasn't worth it."

"I don't think I ever would have told people how I really felt about certain things. Now I can and I will."

"I feel confident enough to get up and speak and know that people will take me seriously."

7 Steps to Fearless Speaking

7 Steps to Fearless Speaking

Lilyan Wilder

John Wiley & Sons, Inc.

New York • Chichester • Weinheim • Brisbane • Singapore • Toronto

At their request, the names of some students and clients mentioned in this book have been changed to respect their privacy and confidentiality.

This book is printed on acid-free paper. ∞

This publication is designed to provide accurate and authoritative information in regard to the subject matter covered. It is sold with the understanding that the publisher is not engaged in rendering legal, accounting, or other professional services. If legal advice or other expert assistance is required, the services of a competent professional person should be sought.

Library of Congress Cataloging-in-Publication Data:
Wilder, Lilyan.
    7 steps to fearless speaking / by Lilyan Wilder.
        p.   cm.
    Includes bibliographical references and index.
    ISBN 0-471-32159-1 (pbk. : alk. paper)
    1. Public speaking.   I. Title.   II. Title: Seven steps to fearless speaking.
PN4121.W3865   1999
808.5'1—dc21   98-55161
                                                            CIP

Printed in the United States of America.

10 9 8 7 6 5 4 3

"Know thyself" was written over the portal of the antique world. Over the portal of the new world, "Be thyself" shall be written.

OSCAR WILDE

CONTENTS

▼

7 Steps to
Fearless Speaking

Introduction

If you asked me what I came into
this world to do, I will tell you: I
came to live out loud.

EMILE ZOLA

Fear of public speaking consistently tops every list of human fears.

In an often-cited 1993 study done by the polling firm Bruskin-Goldring, 45 percent of those surveyed said they feared public speaking. Thirty percent said they feared death.

In a study of 3,000 Americans published in the *Book of Lists* (David Wallechinsky, Little, Brown, 1995), the number one fear cited by 41 percent of those studied was speaking to an audience.

And a similar study by A. Ronald Seifert of the Behavioral Institute of Atlanta indicated that "40 million Americans hate speaking so much, they'd do almost anything to avoid it, and perhaps as many as 40 million who speak all the time feel anxious and do not want to give a talk!"

If you are one of those millions who have been plagued all their lives by fear of public speaking . . . if you feel that fear has impeded your career and diminished your life . . . this book can help you.

The Seven Steps to Fearless Speaking explained in these pages are the culmination of more than 30 years of teaching the art of communication—at the New School for Social Research in New York City, at Columbia University Graduate School of Journalism, at Hunter and Brooklyn Colleges, in private sessions in my studio, and in corporate conference rooms all over America.

The Seven Steps . . .

Experience Your Voice,

Get a Response and Structure Your Thoughts,

Establish a Dialogue,

Tap Your Creativity,

Learn to Persuade,

Achieve Your Higher Objective, and

Give the Gift of Your Conviction

. . . are a road map to a place where you can freely and fearlessly say what you know and what you believe. A place where you can truly be yourself as a public speaker and communicate from the depth of your convictions.

My alumni, who number in the thousands, include broadcasters and businessmen, stockbrokers and senators, homemakers and heads of state. Many of them suffered from fear of speaking. Our work together taught me how to help you.

"Why Are You Here?"

I begin each private session and class by asking the question, "Why are you here?" My students give me answers like these:

"I feel I have limited my life because of my fear of public speaking. I have managed so far to fast-talk my way out of most presentations. But the excuses are running out. I'm tired of living like this."

"I get petrified the night before I have to speak before a group, and can't sleep all night. It's as if no matter what I do, I have no control over my thoughts or body. At the same time, it's something I long to do. Something I want desperately. I envy people who can. I want to be one of those people."

"I get very hoarse in my throat. It's not dryness. . . . I can't eat or drink. I bring the water to my mouth and I can't swallow. . . . Thinking on my feet, when I'm very nervous, all I can think about is how I'm standing in front of a large group of people and they're all paying attention to me. How can I possibly even remember what the person asked?"

"I have spent the last 20 years at work controlling situations and talking my way out of public speaking. I do fine when I choose to enter a conversation, but when I have to get up in front of the group or get called on . . . I've been very good at getting out of it."

My students are of all ages and from all walks of life. Their common denominator is their shared feelings of frustration, fear, and confusion. They confirm the fact that fear of speaking is an equal-opportunity affliction. It does not discriminate because of gender, age, religious belief, socioeconomic class, job description, or ethnic origin.

Fear and the Famous

The famous aren't immune, either. The roster includes James Earl Jones, Barbra Streisand, Carly Simon, Willard Scott, and Maya Angelou.

James Garner, a lifelong sufferer of fear of speaking, once paused during the filming of *The Rockford Files* to admit to a newspaper reporter that he was extremely nervous about delivering an upcoming commencement address at the University of Oklahoma in his hometown of Norman.

"It's been driving me nuts," he said, "thinking about the speech while I'm trying to finish this movie."

Cellist Pablo Casals has had to be physically pushed on stage on several occasions. Once, after injuring his hand while hiking, he happily announced, "Thank God, I'll never have to play the cello again." (Fortunately, the injury wasn't permanent.)

Laurence Olivier is said to have suffered stage fright so acutely, he asked his fellow cast members not to look him in the eye while he was performing.

Thomas Jefferson was terrified of speaking in public and never did overcome it. Near the end of his life, he confided to a friend that he was outraged by what he regarded as the Continental Congress's heavy-handed revision of his carefully written Declaration of Independence—but was unable to speak up and defend his work.

Former First Lady Rosalynn Carter was bedeviled by fear of speaking, too. Most of her life, she managed to avoid public speaking. But as First Lady, she couldn't.

In her autobiography, *The First Lady from Plains* (Houghton Mifflin, 1984), she explains:

> The idea of standing up in front of people absolutely terrified me . . . speeches were impersonal, and I was certain I would be struck dumb if I ever had to make one.

But, on the campaign trail, there was no place to hide. And hiding wasn't her goal. Helping her husband get elected governor of Georgia, and eventually president of the United States, was her goal. So, speak up she did, over and over again:

> I started practicing at small coffees and receptions, making a deliberate decision to say a few words at each. I always arrived very nervous and headed straight for the bathroom, locked myself in, and said my lines (which couldn't have been more than two minutes long) over and over. . . . For a long time it was torture for me. I never knew when I opened my mouth whether any words would come out or not. My knees shook. I was always afraid I would go blank in the middle of my remarks . . .

However, as time passed,

> It got much easier for me . . . and before the campaign was over I was making brief speeches often.

Her fortitude, her careful preparation, and her willingness to go back again and again, practice and practice some more, eventually paid off.

Mrs. Carter triumphed over her fear because her objective was clear and her desire to express her convictions was strong—so strong that her need to say what was on her mind eventually replaced her fear.

Fear and the Real You

There is no relationship between fear of public speaking and personal resourcefulness, education, or imagination.

Far from it. I am continually impressed by the intelligence and creativity of the people who come to me for help, and how much they have to offer. They are CEOs, doctors, lawyers, authors, artists, designers, accountants, financial advisors, computer experts, homemakers active in their communities and their houses of worship, professional volunteers, administrators of charities and nonprofit organizations, architects, and middle-management executives.

They are like you, people who can make a difference. What a shame, then, to hear statements like this, from one of my students: "I had something to say and didn't. I might as well not have been there."

When you don't say what you know and feel, when you withhold yourself, the world is poorer for it.

A Fear Inventory

When you have a speaking chore to face, do you procrastinate? Do you avoid preparing, because to do so just seems to make you more nervous? When you visualize yourself in front of the audience, do any of these thoughts run through your mind?

- "They'll think I don't know what I'm doing."
- "I'll make a fool of myself."
- "I'll look stupid."
- "They'll know more about this than I do."
- "My hands will shake."
- "My voice will crack."
- "They'll think I'm disorganized."
- "I'll go blank."
- "I'll lose my place."
- "I'll be boring."
- "I don't know how to do this."
- "I'm not prepared."
- "I don't know how to prepare."
- "I'm no good at this."
- "I can't do it."
- "They'll ask questions I can't answer."

The Cost of Fear

The toll in lost opportunities and frustration exacted by the fear of speaking is enormous. It can thwart your career advancement. In an era of corporate restructuring and downsizing, it can be the difference between keeping and losing a job.

Face it: If you can't orchestrate a meeting, you're of little use to a corporation.

But the cost runs even deeper than that. It keeps men and women from fulfilling their potential and sharing their unique knowledge, skills, and passions.

Fear of speaking can do the following:

- Lead you to believe you are less competent and worthy than you are.
- Keep your ideas from being heard.
- Keep you from applying for the position you really want.
- Become a glass ceiling on your career.
- Cost you your job in a downsizing or corporate restructuring.

What I Teach and Why

I have devoted my life to teaching people to communicate effectively in public—to overcome fear, to find and use their voices, to plan and say what is on their minds and in their hearts.

The Seven Step Program teaches you to replace fear with a deeper, more meaningful involvement in your message. It is an alternative to the method that uses artificial inflections, mechanical gestures, and any other superficialities.

Realizing the difference between these two methods is what turns an ordinary talking head into a competent broadcast communicator who is listened to, believed, and sought after.

Realizing the difference is what turns a forgettable drone into an effective business speaker whose information and ideas energize his or her listeners.

Realizing the difference is what enables a lifelong fearful speaker to become fearless at last.

Because the Seven Step Program is rooted in human values and not performance mechanics, it is unlike any other you may have undertaken in an effort to overcome your fear of speaking.

In this program, you will *not* be taught to:

- Worry about when and how often to make eye contact with your listeners, as if eye contact were a substitute for making a *real* connection with them.
- Practice putting your hands in and taking them out of your pockets, or using other prescribed gestures for effect.
- Vary your vocal modulation, pitch, and tempo for variation's sake.
- Pretend that your listeners are so many heads of cabbage, or that they are all naked, or some other nonsensical fantasy that denies the reality of one-on-one communication. (One of my students, who stuttered as a child, told me, "People were always giving me brainless advice like that.")

In this program, you *will* be taught to:

- Breathe properly.
- Hear and enjoy your real voice.
- Get an immediate response from your listeners.
- Sustain that response and make your presentation a give-and-take that is as stimulating for you as it is for your listeners.
- Speak, at all times, from your intelligence, experience, and beliefs.

Like all teachers, I had teachers, too. And two of them changed my life. What I learned from them formed the foundation for what I teach.

The first was the late Professor Lew Sarett of Northwestern University, who taught me that an "able speaker" is also an "able person"—a person of character.

"An able speaker," Professor Sarett wrote, "is one who possesses or is achieving the power to speak excellently." At the same time, an able person is one "who possesses or is achieving excellence as a human being, one who is developing his own best potentialities in the art of living."

The able speaker, Professor Sarett taught, has something of value to say and has as his or her purpose the communication of those feelings and ideas "toward the achievement of some productive end."

Recognize yourself as a person of character who has something to say, and what you have to say will become more important than your fear of saying it.

My second great teacher was Lee Strasberg, the immensely influential acting coach whose teachings are still practiced.

As a young actress, I learned from him his famous acting "method," which is based on two liberating emotional exercises: the Private Moment and the Affective Memory. Both are designed to help the actor bring his or her own memories and life experiences to bear on the portrayal of a character. That connection to real life brings a compelling dimension of reality to the performance.

You are not here to learn to act, of course. But bringing your own experience, your own sense of reality to bear on your public speaking connects you to your subject and your audience as nothing else can.

So I adapted both of these exercises to my teaching. They form the basis for the work we will do in Step Seven, Give the Gift of Your Conviction.

The real you as a public speaker is there, behind the fear, just waiting to be brought out. All of the work we are about to undertake together is aimed toward that wonderful objective.

But first, let's talk about the fear that has caused you so much pain.

The Five Fears

What is more mortifying than to
feel that you have missed the plum
for want of courage to shake
the tree?

LOGAN PEARSALL SMITH

Why do you have the fear of speaking?

You've probably asked yourself that question many times and found no satisfactory answer. The only thing you know for sure is what happens when it comes time to speak in public: the panic, the dry throat, the struggle to remember everything you meant to say, the fear that the words might not come.

I know you want to free yourself from that fear forever; that's why you've undertaken this program. Before we begin the cure, however, it will help to know the possible sources of your fear.

I believe there are five basic sources of fear of speaking. They are:

1. Career terror
2. Perfectionism
3. Panic
4. Avoidance
5. Trauma

If you are like most of my students, your fear is rooted in more than one of these areas. Probably two or three. And as we study the Seven Steps, the sources of your fear will become evident.

It's important to understand the nature of each fear. When you can identify a fear as your own, you can begin to lessen the effect of it.

Fear One: Career Terror

As the name suggests, **career terror** is exclusively job-related. It's rooted in the awful feeling that your job, your career, your future is on the line every time you step before a group, enter a meeting, or pick up the telephone.

Many of my students seek my help because they believe their fear of speaking is inhibiting their careers. As a result, they pass up good opportunities and shrink from taking leadership roles, choosing instead jobs that don't require them to speak.

Circumstances that trigger career terror include:

- Being promoted to a higher level of responsibility and feeling enormous pressure to live up to new expectations
- Speaking to a large audience of strangers in an unfamiliar setting
- The presence of a hostile boss or a competitive, intimidating coworker
- Being forced to use prewritten scripts
- Pressure to use the language of the corporation, incorporating into your talk stock phrases and buzzwords that are foreign to the way you really express yourself
- Using unfamiliar new technology, such as videoconferencing
- Being assigned to talk about things you know nothing about
- Not having enough time to prepare

Feeling overwhelmed can cause you to lose faith in yourself, and you suddenly find anxiety snowballing. At that point, even low-stress presentations become occasions for dread and seem insurmountable.

Here's a sampling of experiences of career terror told by some of my students. Do you recognize yourself in any of them?

"I went through hell interviewing for my current job. It was terrifying. I literally sat there holding on to my chair for the entire interview."

"I'm okay one-on-one, but on television I feel a billion people are staring at me. Also, I'm bad at small talk. Bottom line, I can't give a speech to a nine-year-old child."

"I'm very anxious about making this speech. Very anxious. I have to accept an award from the museum. At board meetings, with clients, I'm fine. But the thought of facing one thousand people . . . what do I do about this anxiety?"

"I'm just constantly thrown into situations where I can have a conference call from 10 to 11 and then, boom, I have another one, and some of them are just spur of the moment, you know they're not planned in any way . . . there's not enough time to prepare."

If you see yourself in any of these situations, know that you aren't alone. Career terror is pervasive in the workplace. And its victims are everywhere, from the boardroom to the copy room.

ROD'S STORY
You Can Run, but You Can't Hide

Rod, an account manager at a large insurance corporation, was very afraid of speaking in front of a group. He knew it could hold him back in his company, but he skirted the issue by becoming adept at avoiding speaking situations. Once, however, he was caught off guard:

"I was in a meeting," he told us in class, "and they were going around the room introducing themselves, and I thought, 'Oh, no, how did this happen? How can I get out of it?' I just had to say a sentence or two, but I was terrified.

"The fear got so bad that I left the room right before it was my turn to talk. I just kind of ducked out of the room for a couple of minutes and tried to regain my sanity. I was short of breath and I thought I was going to lose my voice."

Rod headed for the men's room, got a drink of water, and wondered how much damage he had done to himself.

He crept back into the room and joined the meeting in progress. Everyone had noticed his abrupt departure.

"My boss made a comment," he said. "He was fishing for an explanation of why I walked out, but I didn't say anything. I think everyone could see how scared I was.

"He doesn't know I have the fear of speaking. But what difference would it make if he did? What kind of excuse is that for a manager to duck out of a meeting? You don't go to the bathroom right when you're the next person to speak!"

Rod didn't lose his job. But he didn't waste any time getting to class, either. He knew he had to overcome his fear, or the same thing might happen again. And in the process of working through the Seven Steps, he got his career terror under control.

Fear Two: Perfectionism

Perfectionists are usually bright, clever, and successful people who expect nothing less than perfection from themselves.

High standards and high achievement are the upside of **perfectionism.** Obsessive devotion to flawlessness, however, can become a serious obstacle to fearless speaking.

The important thing to remember is that the purpose of public speaking is communication, not perfection. Communicating what you want to say—what you know, think, and feel—is the ultimate goal of the effort. And you can't accomplish that effectively, much less pleasurably, if you are terrified of making even a tiny mistake.

Companies, like individuals, can also be afflicted with perfectionism. Corporations that prize detailed planning and careful organization often cross the line and demand adherence to prepackaged scripts. In so doing, they think they are assuring quality by leaving no stone unturned. But in reality, they are eliminating the one quality that would make the difference between real communication and rote reading—fallible, spontaneous human input of the speaker.

DAVE'S STORY
Mr. Saturday Night Clams Up

Dave, a vice president of sales at a major auto parts supplier, is a charmer who always is the life of any party he attends. In class, he kept us in stitches with his take on life: how hard it is to have a good time; his inadequacies; his very human mistakes, such as getting a rare-breed dog, then finding out his wife can't stand it.

He fulfilled one assignment, a speech about his favorite weekend, with a tale about how he and his wife went to the mountains looking for a summer rental for the family. He also hoped it would turn into a romantic weekend. Instead, the real estate broker didn't leave them alone for two seconds.

Dave memorized and wrote out word for word every speech he made. When there was human frailty in it, he got laughs—and that connected his audiences to him. But when he practiced work-related material in class, the speeches were mechanical.

When Dave told stories about his family's adventures, he was relaxed and fearless. But the speeches he prepared for work changed him into a different person.

The on-the-job Dave was superserious. When I tried to take his written words away from him Dave and I had a tug-of-war with the paper his speech was written on. I told him I wanted to help him experience what it's like to think on his feet, to get a response, to enjoy give-and-take with his audience, and he literally became red in the face.

"Write everything out and then not say it?" he asked, wide-eyed. "Aren't we supposed to say everything we prepared to say? Everything I have written down?"

Driven by his perfectionism, he was petrified at the thought of making some slip-up, forgetting some detail. He allowed no chance for spontaneity or for the humor that made his personal tales so winning.

Eventually, Dave came to understand that when he was speaking to his employees about meeting next month's distribution quota he didn't have to be a stiff, executive type. He could dialogue with them. That helped to unleash his humor. He was able to trade in his "perfect" script for a brief outline that guided him in an enjoyable give-and-take with his staff. The real Dave began to emerge on the job, as well as in casual situations.

Fear Three: Panic

My students tell me that their fear is often exacerbated by their own negative thoughts. They listen to the voices in their heads, telling them they'll make fools of themselves, or that they know less or are less than the audience they want to connect with.

Worse, they worry about very real physical manifestations of their fear—that their hands will shake or their voices crack. I call it the **panic** spiral, as illustrated in the following story.

RHONDA'S STORY
A Fearful Show-and-Tell

Rhonda, a professional photographer, laughed a lot. But it didn't take long to detect that it was nervous laughter masking real fear.

When I went around the room and asked each student why he or she was taking the course, Rhonda could barely get the words out, and those words that came out were blurred by sounds of laughter.

"I'm so nervous," Rhonda spurted out as she giggled and breathed heavily, "I can't catch my breath. I just . . . want to be able . . . to speak in public."

For the first assignment, which was to talk about something you enjoy doing, Rhonda brought in a big book of photographs that she had taken. The photographs were evocative black-and-white New York street scenes, taken in various seasons and at various times of the day.

Rhonda placed the book on a table in front of the lectern and leaned over the lectern as she spoke. As she pressed herself against the lectern tightly, the lectern pressed against her diaphragm and obstructed her breathing.

Her voice was faint, almost a whisper. She began to explain what she does as a photographer. It was evident that she didn't have control of her sound. The panic spiral began.

Because her anticipation was so strong, her voice became inaudible. When she heard her voice failing, she became more scared. It was hard for her to breathe because her diaphragm was squeezed in. She didn't know how to take deep breaths using her diaphragm and stomach muscles in a productive way. Her legs weakened.

She turned to me and said, "I've got to sit down!"

There was a chair behind her and I suggested she sit in it. She completed her speech from the chair.

That was how the panic spiral worked on Rhonda. Anticipation created a physical reaction. That physical response led to more insecurity. That escalated her heart rate and she found it hard to breathe. She went blank and her knees buckled.

A few weeks into the Seven Step Program, Rhonda was telling her story much more easily—and having fun doing it.

She was learning to breathe properly, to enjoy the sound of her voice. And she had discovered how stimulating it is to get and maintain a response from her listeners.

We looked at Rhonda's photographs again, and this time the presentation took on a refreshing new dimension for us: Rhonda was by then able to tell us the story behind each fascinating snapshot of daily life in our city.

We had many questions, and Rhonda was delighted to answer them. Her head was full of her story, not her fear. The panic spiral was thwarted before it began.

Fear Four: Avoidance

In the musical, *You're a Good Man, Charlie Brown,* the procrastinating hero frets over a book report he must give to the class in two days. Should he do it now or wait until tomorrow?

"I'll wait 'til tomorrow," he sings comically. "I work best under pressure, and there'll be lots of pressure . . . if I wait 'til tomorrow. . . ."

Charlie Brown's **avoidance** of preparation for his oral book report provided a funny moment in a delightful show. But the reality of avoidance—its potential consequences in your life—is no laughing matter.

Avoidance is a problem shared by many. It is self-sabotage that virtually guarantees anxiety, fear, and diminished performance. If you're not sure of what you're saying, it is obvious. Your listeners know it—just as you would in their position.

So the answer is, just get with the program and do your homework, right?

Well, for many people, it's not that easy. Avoidance has its roots in other fears. Careless as you may think you are, you may really be a perfectionist at heart, setting impossible standards for yourself that scare you.

Or you may be afraid of committing to take the first step toward making a speech: just picking up a pen and paper to compose a speech. Sometimes people are simply afraid to start because that means "I'll have to follow through." You justify delaying by thinking, "One more television show right after this movie . . . I'll read a while to prime the pump . . . lunch first, then work . . . got to walk the dog . . . maybe I'll get up really early in the morning. . . ."

Psychologist Karen Horney's study of self-esteem yielded this encouraging result: When a person attempts something, intellectually or physically, he or she usually succeeds. Yet most people imagine they will fail more often than succeed and never attempt what they want to do.

The result, she explains, is that "what we do not attempt to do out of fear is experienced as failure."

You're scared. You avoid. And you're more convinced than ever that you aren't capable.

JEANETTE'S STORY
Avoiding Work by Fighting Dirt

Jeanette, who worked at the ASPCA, was so obsessed with procrastinating that she literally cleaned her house from top to bottom to avoid sitting down to create a speech for class.

The subject was "Your Favorite Weekend." She finally wrote the speech about how she avoided writing the speech. Here's how she characterized her avoidance:

> I sat down and thought of every weekend since my youth. I couldn't come up with anything, so I decided what I really needed was a cup of coffee. I poured myself a cup and reached into the refrigerator for some milk and I suddenly noticed the refrigerator was a mess. So I threw away all the old food and wiped down the shelves.
>
> Then I told myself, "Stop, enough distraction. Let's get back to work." I sat back down on the couch. I doodled for a while until I finally dropped my pencil and leaned over to pick it up. When I did, I realized the living room floor was really kind of dirty. Twenty minutes later I had vacuumed and mopped the floor. As I was pouring the bucket of water into the toilet, I saw that it, too, needed to be cleaned, as well as the sink and the tub.

By the time Jeanette had finished—about midnight—she had painted her bathroom. It wasn't until the following day, after she had seen her therapist and he had urged her to just do it and even consider writing "a bad speech, not so great a speech," that she actually sat down again and completed her speech.

She heard the class's laughter as she described her avoidance pattern and how she ended up cleaning and painting her apartment. But she learned a lesson, too: that taking pen in hand to put a speech together makes that speech a reality. It's a commitment. It's concrete. It can scare you. But once you're over that hurdle, you're on your way.

After that initial breakthrough, she gave many sensitive and original speeches. And the memory of her procrastination speech lived on, a reminder to us all.

Avoidance is easy to kid about, but, again, I urge you to take it seriously and to be honest with yourself about your preparation habits. Preparation is one of the keys to fearless speaking.

If avoidance is a major source of fear for you, face it. Make yourself turn on the computer, pick up the pen, and put some words on paper. Respect yourself and your audience by knowing that what you have to say and how you want to say it is valuable.

Fear Five: Trauma

Sometimes, the fear of speaking is rooted in the memory of something terrible that happened to you in the past. It could be a specific incident or a continuing experience.

If you feel that your fear of speaking is related to childhood **trauma** or painful past conditioning, professional counseling can be very helpful. Facing the trauma and understanding its impact on you can trigger a breakthrough to help overcome the fear of speaking.

Victims of trauma patterning are people who were told, over and over, by parents or other adults, that they weren't capable enough— they were stupid, dull, homely, clumsy, doomed to fail. Consequently, they became conditioned to fear humiliation, ridicule, parental anger, a teacher's negative assessments of them, and the resulting hurt feelings. They find it less painful and easier to simply not speak, to just hide, to stay mute.

Or if you grew up exposed to physical, verbal, or emotional abuse; the death of a parent; or the rejection of a loved one, your fear of speaking may originate in these memories. You need to bring to the surface those experiences that you internalized and face them for what they did to you.

Here's an example of how a childhood trauma plagued me well into adulthood.

MY PERSONAL TRAUMA
The Death of Unconditional Love

There was a time in my life when I was mute. My father died when I was 13. Though I knew that something tragic had occurred, I didn't realize the full impact his death had on me for many years. I know that I shut down. I did not talk except to express immediate needs and answer questions that had to be answered. I didn't talk. When people tried to communicate with me, I clammed up. My jaw was locked. I stared into space. I did not respond.

At one point, when I was fifteen, I went to the emergency room at Cook County Hospital in Chicago where I lived. After a long wait, I saw a doctor. I told him I didn't feel alive. "I feel dead," I said. He raised the sleeve of the navy blue sweater my mother had knitted for me and he pinched my arm. He asked, "Do you feel that?" I said, "Yes." He said, "You're alive," and he dismissed me.

Gradually, through life experiences like reading, going to college, and developing friendships, but mainly through being in the theater and acting, I began to open up. Performing on stage, experiencing my inner life through the characters I portrayed, was more real to me than my real life. Little by little, I found myself and my voice. I began to speak more freely.

This experience helped me develop a deep feeling of compassion for people who find it difficult to speak. Maya Angelou experienced a trauma that muted her. She was raped, then required to identify her attacker in court and listen to the sentencing that followed. These events forced her to question the wisdom of speaking at all. James Earl Jones, too, suffered an early event that caused him to shut down. Although not rooted in violence, his trauma—a family move from his home in the South to a white community in Michigan—has stayed with him. To this day, he stutters when he is feeling stress.

I believe that all stoppages of speech—whether their origins are traumatic, physical, or the result of neglect by well-meaning elders—

produce the same frustrating effect. This is true even of the sort of deliberate mumbling people sometimes use to evade intelligibility. The feelings of choking, resentment, anger, and despair are powerful. Whether we call it fear of speaking, stage fright, or panic, it hurts. It stops us from living, exploring, enjoying, worshipping, appreciating, observing—everything.

Let's Get Started

If I have the belief that I can do it,
I shall surely acquire the capacity to
do it even if I may not have it at
the beginning.

MAHATMA GANDHI

Because I am a teacher, I write the way I teach. I want this book to duplicate, insofar as possible, the experience you would receive in my class, in a self-help workshop, in my office, or in a conference room. This book is your guide.

The path to fearless speaking is a series of steps. Each step:

- Builds on the step before it
- Incorporates the principles of the step that precedes it
- Begins with relaxation, breathing, and vocalization exercises
- Culminates in a speaking assignment
- Has a self-critique questionnaire
- Leads to improvement

You'll start with one-on-one presentations and work your way up to larger groups.

Doing the Work

I want to emphasize the importance of your willingness and discipline to do the work required in this Seven Step Program.

When I was writing the proposal for this book, I wanted to title it *7 Weeks to Fearless Speaking*. An agent—only half in jest, I later surmised—told me I would have a better chance of selling the book if I called it *7 Minutes to Fearless Speaking.*

Well, even if I could sell more books titled *7 Seconds, 7 Minutes,* or even *7 Days to Fearless Speaking,* I wouldn't do it. I wouldn't promise you such a miracle.

This book is titled *7 Steps to Fearless Speaking,* and that is just what it offers. The method is based on my classroom and private teaching, but it is self-taught: You serve as your own coach—and go at your own speed.

But do not expect to go through this program with little or no effort and get results. To offer you snake oil would be a disservice to you and disrespectful to all the people who have made themselves into fearless speakers.

One of the biggest misconceptions about public speaking is that those who are best at it are "naturals" who don't need practice. We should know better; after all, we recognize that star athletes and musicians practice endlessly. So why not the best public speakers? Excellent performers and speakers end up looking "natural" and "real" precisely because they have practiced and worked out the kinks.

So it was with Ronald Reagan, the Great Communicator. When he spoke in public, it looked effortless. But Reagan spent hours rehearsing for a press conference. For a major speech, he'd close his doors and spend at least 12 hours practicing out loud.

People who speak, or play tennis or the piano, effortlessly are the very people who work the hardest. Billie Jean King, the great tennis pro, in addition to spending every waking hour she could on the tennis court, had a tennis ball hanging down from the ceiling above her bed. She would focus on the ball before falling asleep at night. She did not take her eye off the ball in bed or on the tennis court.

How to Use This Book

The value of this book is that it offers you two ways to study the Seven Step Program:

1. You can use it alone and be your own coach.
2. You can organize a self-help workshop and go through the program with others.

And, for those of you who bought this book in desperation, looking for help with the speech you must give three days or three hours from now, there are an Emergency Kit and a First Aid Kit, which will help you. These tips will help you through a crisis, but they are not intended as substitutes for the Seven Steps.

How to Be Your Own Coach

When you are your own coach, you can work at your own speed, set your own speaking schedule, go back and work through earlier steps several times if you choose.

The downside is that you don't have a teacher or a group to react to you. When you work alone, you will need to find places to speak in order to fulfill the assignments. And you will need to motivate yourself, as a coach would do. For example:

- Audiotape and play back your practice sessions.
- Get your spouse, partner, or friend to give you feedback as you practice.
- Provide self-inspiration by pinning affirmations, quotations, photographs of successful communicators to your wall.
- After you've given the speech, reward yourself with an activity you've been putting off, like going to a movie you've been wanting to see for weeks or getting that book you've been wanting to read.

One of the greatest pitfalls of the self-coached approach, however, is the temptation to succumb to the old fear, put the book aside, and procrastinate. If you feel yourself pulled in this direction, here are some ways to stay on track:

- Reread the section on avoidance in the preceding chapter.
- Make a list of all the reasons you are not doing the assignment. What, exactly, are you afraid of?
- Then make a list of everything you stand to gain if you become a fearless speaker: You will do better in your career, your friends and family will be proud of you, and, most important of all, you will feel so much better being free at last from the fear that has dogged you for so long.

How to Organize a Self-Help Workshop

In a self-help workshop, you'll proceed with the Seven Steps with others in the group who are working through them at the same time. You'll all be using this book as your guide and workbook.

The only drawback to this approach may be scheduling. Regular meetings of busy people are hard to organize. But if you and your fellow workshop members are motivated to complete the program, you will make the time.

Here's how to proceed:

- Put a note on the bulletin board of your workplace: "Anyone interested in joining a self-help program called 'Seven Steps to Fearless Speaking,' call _____."
- Put a similar notice in the monthly newsletter of your place of worship.
- Start a chat group online.
- Advertise in a local community newspaper. The cost is minimal or free. Here's an announcement I have run several times:

  Are you interested in reaching your potential as a public speaker? Do you want to conquer your fear of speaking? Join a Self-Help Workshop to follow a tested program called "Seven Steps to Fearless Speaking." The cost is minimal. Call _____.

When you get a response, make a date to meet one person at a time. Have a copy of *7 Steps to Fearless Speaking* with you. Tell the prospective participants about the program. Ask why they want to be part of the group. Explain that it's a commitment, but the results are positive.

Choose five people in addition to yourself. Select a place to meet: your home, a church, a synagogue, an office, a conference room at work. Many companies encourage people to gather for communication skills training and will provide a meeting place.

Plan to meet for 90 minutes once a week for seven weeks. Each participant should buy this book and read the introductory chapters and Step One prior to the first meeting.

The meeting place should have chairs and a lectern or table for the speaker's notes. Each person should bring a tape recorder to record his or her speaking assignment at each session and the discussion that follows it.

Appoint one person to be the workshop facilitator, to start the meetings and preside, and one person to be the timekeeper.

Each chapter takes you step by step through the instructions and the assignments.

At the first session, arrange the chairs in a circle so you are facing each other. Go around the room and introduce yourselves: your name, occupation, where you are from.

Each person should answer the questions, "Why are you here? and "What do you hope to get out of this self-help program?"

Now, each person should take a moment to reflect on this question: "Let's say you go to Heaven tomorrow, and St. Peter, Moses, or Allah meets you at the Pearly Gates and asks you, 'What have you done in your life that you are most proud of?' Or, 'What is the one thing that you think is most special about you?' "

Go around the room and have each person answer. Here are some real-life examples from my students:

> "I ran the New York Marathon. I have been overweight all my life, and running the marathon helped strengthen my new-found courage to keep my weight off."

> "I produced a three-minute segment on the bells of Riverside Church for the *Today* show. It was an especially tricky shoot to coordinate, but I pulled it off. It was my first national exposure."

> "I took care of a friend who was dying of AIDS. He had always been there for me when I needed him, and it was important for me to be there for him, too."

When everyone has finished, congratulate yourselves. Realize that you have just given a short speech. You have spoken in public, and you have shared something meaningful to you with others. That is the essence of communication—finding meaning in what you say, and then sharing it with others."

Tools You'll Need

Whether you choose to be your own coach or to be part of a self-help workshop, before you begin, assemble the tools you'll need to help you complete the program.

This Book

You will need a copy of *7 Steps to Fearless Speaking*.

Tape Recorder

The tape recorder need not be expensive, but you should buy one that takes standard cassettes, not microcassettes. Since you will be recording and listening to your own voice, you want a tape recorder that has good sound reproduction. Otherwise, you will not get an accurate playback of your voice. And if you stick with the standard cassettes, you can play your recordings in your car as you drive.

Two Notebooks

You will carry one notebook with you at all times to jot down thoughts and ideas as they come to you. Choose one you can carry in a coat pocket or in your purse. It could be a reporter's notebook. You also should have a full-size notebook in which to organize your outlines and complete the exercises in this book.

Start a File

Clip and save articles from newspapers and magazines on subjects that relate to your interests and professional expertise. Good background files often can make the difference between being fully prepared or not. "Instant erudition," one of my students calls his file. A box of manila folders or an accordion file is useful. And I'm sure you'll make use of the best reference source and filing system of all: the Internet and your computer.

Look for Places to Speak

In the self-help workshop you have a built-in audience. But if you are being your own coach, begin looking for places to speak. As you go through the Seven Step Program, you'll need to become your own speakers bureau.

But almost everywhere you go socially presents an opportunity to practice. So redefine your outings as speaking opportunities. These may include cocktail parties, dinner parties, lunches. Practice one or two of the Seven Steps by slipping them into the exchange of conversation at these times. Volunteer to speak before committees, community groups, church groups. Raise your hand high in class, and be sure you are called on. Attend a town council meeting and speak up.

Acknowledge and believe that you are a person of intelligence and authority, a thoughtful, insightful person whose views are wanted and appreciated. In other words, as my professor, Lew Sarett, said, "Believe you have something of value to say." The time to start saying it is now.

▼

Experience Your Voice

*Voices—I think they must go
deeper into us than other things.
I have often fancied heaven might
be made of voices.*

GEORGE ELIOT

Your voice is your fingerprint. It produces a sound that is distinctively yours. It belongs to you, and no one else.

That sound says as much about you as the words you choose. Produced confidently and fully, it can be the mirror of your soul. Produced carelessly, it can detract from what you have to say and even undermine you.

The first step toward fearless speaking, then, is to learn to produce a strong, relaxed voice that is easy to listen to, lively, and compelling. That voice is within you now. It just needs to be set free and kept healthy.

Before anyone else can enjoy your voice, you must learn to enjoy it yourself. To discover its true quality, its range, its power, its subtleties. To feel the strength and fearlessness that come with the free flow of your own sound.

In order to develop your own sound, you need to find it. That means recognizing and accepting your natural voice. You may not sound like James Earl Jones, or Diane Sawyer, or Charles Osgood. You will sound like you. There is a wide range of sound you can explore.

In this chapter, you will begin the search for your true voice. You will learn to relax, to breathe properly, and to produce a pleasing, resonant sound.

I am passionate about this and cannot overemphasize the importance of the work you will do in this chapter. The relaxation, breathing, and vocal exercises you will learn in this step form the foundation for the work you will do in the next six steps.

The quality of the sound you produce depends on what you do with your body, mind, and soul. Let's start with your body.

If you are tense, that tension affects your vocal cords. If your breathing is shallow, your voice will be thin and weak, and you won't have enough breath to get you through to the ends of sentences.

The relaxation exercise in this first step will become your preparation, your warm-up for each new step of the program. No athlete would plunge into the demands of play without first warming up, preparing both physically and mentally. Nor should you, as a speaker.

In many years of teaching and coaching, I've found that my students, almost without exception, can improve their sound. And when they do, they are delighted to reclaim something they had lost long ago—breathing in a relaxed way like a baby.

The relationship between your voice and your body is organic. At the moment of your birth, when you inhaled and noisily expelled your first breath, your voice and your body were naturally in harmony.

Somewhere, somehow, we've fallen off the track. Before we can get back on, we must relearn what babies know instinctively. Watch how a baby breathes, and you'll see what I mean. The baby uses its stomach and diaphragm to inhale and exhale. More about that later.

How James Earl Jones Found His Voice

When I ask my students whose voices they admire, many say James Earl Jones. The actor's rich, rolling baritone is as familiar to everyone as the voice of a family member or dear friend.

He's the screen voice of Darth Vader in the *Star Wars* trilogy, the father lion in *The Lion King,* the ubiquitous television spokesman for the telephone company. Theatergoers recall his great voice reaching every seat in the house in the varied roles he's played: Jack Jefferson, the fiery boxer in *The Great White Hope;* the title role in *Othello;* Paul Robeson, as a one-man show; Sam, the South African servant in *Master Harold . . . and the Boys;* Troy Maxon, the angry ex-baseball player in *Fences*. His numerous film appearances include *Field of Dreams* and *Coming to America.*

Jones spent most of his formative years profoundly afraid to speak. He stuttered as a child and withdrew into silence until a knowing high school teacher drew him out.

In his autobiography, *Voices and Silences* (James Earl Jones and Penelope Niven, Charles Scribner & Sons, 1993), he tells how he wrote a poem about the taste of grapefruit, patterned after Longfellow's "Song of Hiawatha": "I forced my grapefruit rhapsody into Longfellow's cadence and rhyme scheme," he writes. "Fortunately, no copy of that poem survives."

Young James Earl was proud of the poem. His teacher, Professor Crouch—seeing an opportunity to break down the wall of silence the student had built around himself—pretended to suspect the work was not original.

"My honor was at stake," Jones writes. "Plagiarism was bad business. I had written every word of the poem myself."

Professor Crouch challenged him to prove it by reciting the poem to the class on the spot.

"It would be a trauma to open my mouth in front of my classmates, who would probably laugh at my poem and my stuttering," he writes. "But it would be a greater trauma to be disgraced, unfairly charged with plagiarism . . .

"I was shaking as I stood up, cursing myself. I strained to get the words out, pushing from the bottom of my soul. I opened my mouth—and to my astonishment, the words flowed out smoothly, every one of them . . ."

Jones described this experience as his breakthrough. For the first time, he experienced his own voice, getting a sense of its capacity for depth of feeling and musicality. He was elated—and hooked.

He practiced by reading Shakespeare aloud in the farm fields that surrounded his rural home, filling the countryside with soliloquies and orations, acting out some of the scenes he would later perform professionally on the stage.

"I would have glorious experiences reading Edgar Allan Poe aloud," he writes. "I could throw back the curtains in the high school gymnasium, step out on the stage with a lighted candle, and read Edgar Allan Poe—and everybody would listen."

A word of caution is in order here for those of you who stutter. The experience Jones had in high school was a breakthrough for him as a stutterer, but it was not a miracle cure for his stuttering. He had to continue to work long and hard to overcome it. Nor am I suggesting that any of the work we will do in this program will "cure" stuttering. But I know from long experience that it will help.

The door Jones opened with the help of his teacher is the same one you will open now. When he learned to experience the joy of his own sound, it changed his life.

Later in this program, you will have the opportunity to practice in the same way Jones practiced, reciting poetry that will enable you to learn to like the sound of your own voice.

How Do You Really Feel about Your Voice?

You must experience your voice in order to know its true power. And that takes time and practice.

Let's begin by assessing how you really feel about your voice. Answer the questions in the following inventory and record them in your notebook.

A VOCAL INVENTORY

1. Do you feel that your voice is pleasing?
2. Does hearing your voice fill you with a sense of confidence and power?
3. Do you feel your voice is meek and you don't get heard?
4. Do people continually ask you to repeat yourself?
5. Do you frequently feel frustrated because people do not respond to you with the respect that you think you deserve?
6. When you speak in public, does your voice fade? Does it have a ruffle or a quiver?
7. Does your voice get choked when you speak in public?
8. Does your voice get hoarse after you speak for 30 minutes?
9. Do you feel your throat is restricted?
10. Do you feel your voice is a true representation of who you are?

Now put the notebook away.

In six or seven weeks, when you have practiced the exercises in Steps One through Seven, I'll ask you to get out the notebook, answer the questions again, and compare those answers to your original ones. I think you'll see quite a difference!

Where Your Sound Comes From

The sound of your voice is the product of air passing through your vocal cords. Your vocal cords are simply muscles, and by keeping them toned and using them correctly, a wide range of sounds becomes possible.

Many people breathe in reverse. By that I mean they pull in their abdomens when they inhale. This works against the natural action of the diaphragm, which should expand along with the abdominal cavity when you inhale. As students of yoga understand, the more efficiently you use your diaphragm and abdominal muscles, the more breath you have. The more breath you have, the better your sound will be.

As suggested earlier, watch how a baby breathes. It automatically expands the abdomen and diaphragm when inhaling and contracts them when exhaling. It's on the exhalation that sound occurs. Crying, cooing, speaking.

The diaphragm is a large muscle attached to the bottom of your rib cage on its periphery. During exhalation, the diaphragm relaxes into a half-moon shape, its natural position of rest. Through the combined movement of the diaphragm and the abdominal muscles, the air moves up from the lungs and through the trachea into the bony cartilage of the throat where the vocal cords (also known as the vocal folds) are located. As the air moves past the cords, they vibrate. These vibrations, or sound waves, are propelled through the four resonating chambers—chest, throat, mouth, and nose—where they become fuller, richer, and more resonant. Finally, the tongue and jaw shape the sound waves into words.

Breathing from the diaphragm comes naturally. Babies have faith in their diaphragms, and you must, too! They automatically inhale. They exhale instinctively. We adults need to learn to breathe again like we did when we were babies, for diaphragmatic breathing is the foundation of good sound.

The Relaxation Response

As it happens, diaphragmatic breathing is also the key to overcoming the shakes, the jitters, the wobblies,—all the myriad responses to fear that our bodies have. Deep, diaphragmatic breathing counteracts the panic response described earlier. It quiets the racing heart, calms the muscles, and slows the flow of adrenaline. The following exercises will teach you how to breathe deeply and further the benefits of that breathing by consciously freeing your muscles of excess tension. This way you can train your body to respond to fear, not with tension, but with relaxation.

Exercise One: Learn to Relax

Concentrate on letting go of all your muscular tension, clearing your mind, focusing only on your breathing.

Tension inhibits inhalation and exhalation. If you're tense, it's difficult to inhale sufficient air and exhale with control. It literally stops your mental, emotional, and sensory experiences. It's like trying to move a baby grand piano and multiplying 384×18 at the same time. You can't do it.

In the same way, it's very difficult to explain your marketing strategy to a roomful of executives while fighting to control the tremor in your voice. Or to convince your fellow taxpaying parents that your children's school needs art and music education, while struggling to get enough breath to get through a sentence.

You can't ever say what you want to say, the way you really want to say it, while your body is constricted with such tension. But there is hope. You can banish the tension and learn to keep it at bay using the following relaxation technique.

Use this technique before you have a presentation to make, a negotiation to conclude, or an overwhelming situation. It will free your mind—and your voice.

If, like so many people, you've been conditioned to "suck in your gut" when you inhale, doing it the right way will take practice. You've been forcing your body to do something it won't do by itself. Now, just relax and feel what happens naturally. You can and should practice proper breathing everywhere and anywhere.

EXERCISE ONE: LEARN TO RELAX

Slump back in your chair as if you were going to fall asleep. Let everything go. Let your arms hang at your sides, your legs stretch out in front of you, your head drop forward. Let your jaw relax. Feel all the tension drain out of your brow. Focus on tension, wherever you feel it. Say to yourself, silently, "Let go." If you feel like letting out some sound—a sigh or a laugh—do so. If you find yourself beginning to giggle, if your eyes tear, or if you drool, don't worry. It means you are becoming more relaxed. Continue relaxing in this position for three to four minutes. Yawn. Open your throat. Feel the soft palate go up and the back of the tongue go down. (This happens automatically when you yawn.) Luciano Pavarotti practices this exercise every day to get resonance into his sound. Let a deep "Ah" sound come out. Then slowly sit up. Open your eyes, and stand up slowly.

Exercise Two: Learn to Breathe Properly

To help concentrate on this new experience, do five-minute segments of this exercise while you walk, drive, ride a bus or train, or watch television. Try to do this every chance you get. Not only will it help you learn to breathe properly, this exercise will help you to relax, slow down, and relieve your tension.

EXERCISE TWO: LEARN TO BREATHE PROPERLY

Place your hand on your midriff and inhale deeply. You will feel the diaphragm and stomach expand like a bellows. Exhale, and they contract. You may inhale and exhale silently through your nose or you may inhale and exhale silently through your mouth. Do this exercise three times in a series of 10 breaths each.

Exercise Three: AIRobics for the Voice

Now, let's practice vocalizing. Using relaxation and proper breathing to produce your sound, do this counting and breathing exercise as part of a 15-minute routine at least once a day.

EXERCISE THREE: AIROBICS FOR THE VOICE

1. *Projection*
   Focus on a spot far away.
   Try to get your voice to reach that spot.

2. *Support*
   Place one hand on your stomach and one hand on your
   diaphragm. Feel them expand, then pull your abdominal
   muscle *in* and your diaphragm *up,* saying:

   ONE!   w—UH—n   (one word on one breath)

   Do the same on each number, slowly, lingering on the vowels:

   TWO!   t—OO

   THREE!   thr—EE

   FOUR!   f—AW—r

   FIVE!   f—I—v

   Nothing but the abdomen and diaphragm should move.
   Shoulders and chest are steady.

3. *Vowels extended*
   Now, count to five on one breath, lingering on the vowels,
   pulling the diaphragm and abdomen in slowly to use up all
   of the air and all of the time it takes to say five words.
   Repeat the count, continuing to breathe properly. Think of
   the vowels as a river with the sound flowing forward, and the
   consonants as the banks of the river containing the sound.

4. *Cheeks up—mouth wide*
   Keeping your cheek muscles up and your mouth widened
   (not lengthened) in a slight smile automatically gives you
   better articulation. Also, it makes you look more alert.

5. *Pitch low*
   A warm, mellow pitch is preferable to a high pitch or nasal
   sound.

6. *Throat open*
   Keeping your throat open, the back of your tongue down,
   and the soft palate raised, as they were when you were
   yawning, creates a resonating chamber for your voice.

> Now, put it all together in this sequence of counts. Concentrate on all six techniques at the same time:
>
> ONE through FIVE (on one breath), then double the tempo
>
> ONE through TEN (on one breath), then triple the tempo
>
> ONE through FIFTEEN (on one breath), then finally try to get all the numbers
>
> ONE through TWENTY (on one breath)

While this exercise may seem a bit overwhelming, do not underestimate the importance of it. If you skimmed over it, stop now, go back, and do it thoughtfully and slowly.

Mastery of the exercises is essential. Like actors, singers, dancers, and athletes who perform certain exercises to warm up before a performance or a game, we will repeat these relaxation, breathing, and vocal exercises before doing each step from now on. Do not try to shortcut them or circumvent them. You want to get to the point where breathing is as natural for speaking as it is for life.

In the next step you will start recording yourself on a tape recorder so you can test whether you are doing the exercises correctly. The objective is to have your sound surround the person you're speaking to and to articulate clearly.

Practice these voice exercises for 15 minutes every day. As we progress, I'll give you a suggested study program, including selections from plays, novels, and poetry. You'll be amazed at what your voice can do. (Consult the Selected Readings for a list of my favorites. Add your own to the list.)

Imagine that you are learning to play the piano. At this point you are practicing scales and drills—but one day "Polonaise" will emerge from your fingertips! You are laying a foundation for the development of your sound—a sound that will consistently connect you to your own power when you get up to speak in public.

And with the power to speak comes the power to express who you really are. To speak up for what you believe and know.

Savor Good Sound

Begin to surround yourself with good, full, vibrant sounds. Do yourself a favor and mix some Frank Sinatra and Ella Fitzgerald, some Mozart and Verdi, in with your usual listening fare. Go to the library and check out recordings of Dylan Thomas and other poets reading their own work. Focus on the voices of the broadcasters you most admire—Ted Koppel, Oprah Winfrey, and Ed Bradley have voices that make me pay attention to them. The more you listen to good sound, the more that sound resonates through your body and helps to bring out the richness in your own voice.

You can't become a fearless speaker until you develop a sound that pleases and supports you. Finding a voice you can rely on—strengthening it or simply getting to know what it can do—will give you a centeredness and self-assurance as a speaker. Knowing that your sound reflects your intelligence and experience diminishes your fear of speaking.

Your Voice and the Real You

Your voice has three components: your actual, unique sound (body); those words that express your real intentions (mind); and your convictions and the sum of your life experience that has made you the person you are (soul).

You begin your study of the Seven Steps by learning to relax, learning to breathe, learning to experience and enjoy rich tones that you didn't know you could produce. But I want you to understand now that producing this sound is not an end in itself.

When you know what you're saying and you believe in it, it affects the tone of your voice. Yes, you have to do the voice exercises; they are essential. But you can do all the voice exercises in the world, and if you don't connect with your inner core, you're not going to have a voice that moves people.

This is the basis of the Seven Step Program. And in the chapters to come, we will explore it in depth.

To show you what you can look forward to, I want to tell you about Carmen, who found her real voice—and Ellen, who doesn't take one breath for granted.

CARMEN'S STORY
The Voice of Authority

For more than 20 years, Carmen was a New York City police officer. She earned a college degree, going to school part-time, and rose to the rank of detective. She often worked undercover. At those times, her high-pitched voice and thick Bronx accent was an asset.

Then Carmen retired from the force and took a job in corporate security, working for one of the largest communications companies in the country. She rose quickly to management level and today has 200 people working for her.

She came to me for help because the Bronx dialect that once served her so well had become, she believed, a hindrance. She had become afraid to speak at work. To her surprise, this brave woman was developing a case of career terror.

"I have to do at least one training session a month," she said. "And also I have to meet with executives. And I just don't sound like the real me. I sound like someone with no education. So I get very tense the minute I have to open my mouth."

When I met Carmen, she was still saying "dem" and "duh" instead of "them" and "the," "lowah" instead of "lower," "haf" instead of "have." She split many words into extra syllables, saying "ster-ong" instead of "strong."

She's very petite, and she spoke in a high-pitched voice—traits that combined to hamper her sense of authority. She was miserable with her sound.

In six months of work together, Carmen reduced her accent 50 percent by practicing exercises to strengthen her tongue and differentiate between the two "TH" sounds and "D" and "T." We also worked on the "R" and "V" sounds. And she learned not to split one-syllable words into two syllables.

We discovered that Carmen's tight, high-pitched sound masked a rich, full voice. When she began doing relaxation work and using deep breathing to produce her voice, her sound strengthened and became more resonant. Now she has a mellow, mature voice that is a voice of authority and that projects to the back of the room.

"I don't feel so nervous now," she says. "When I speak, my voice sounds like me, not some stranger from a long time ago. And I can say what I mean and not be afraid that they're thinking, 'She doesn't know what she's talking about,' because of my accent. I know there is nothing holding me back now."

ELLEN'S STORY
Good Sound despite Multiple Sclerosis

Ellen Burstein, a veteran broadcast journalist and friend of mine, has a very good voice. She also has a severe case of multiple sclerosis and is immobile from the neck down. If you heard her voice on the telephone or on the radio, you would never guess she has a physical handicap. In fact, her voice is better than those of a lot of the people I teach in broadcasting.

She explained that the value of her voice training and the use of her lungs and diaphragm play an important part in the sound of her voice today.

I asked, "What do you do to maintain good sound?"

She replied, "Remember, Lilyan, I was a broadcast journalist for 20 years. As an investigative reporter on television and radio, I had to speak with clarity, precision, and conviction. When MS interrupted my life and I could no longer use my hands to talk and point, a strong voice became even more essential.

"I use a medical device called a spirometer, to strengthen my diaphragm muscles and increase my lung capacity, which had dropped to 25 percent after I had pneumonia. I 'sip and puff' [breathe in and out] through a plastic tube to move my electric wheelchair, control my environment and computer, which I operate with my voice."

I asked, "And that exercises your breathing muscles, the abdomen and the diaphragm?"

"Yes," she said. "I 'sip' to recline my wheelchair and 'puff' to put it upright again. I try to make this action one long breath which strengthens my lung capacity. I need a strong voice to communicate, and it's essential for me to maintain this ability. If I have an exacerbation [of MS], it's the first thing I'll lose."

I tell this story, not only because I admire Ellen for her bravery and unflagging professionalism, but to make a point about how powerful your breathing mechanism can be when you exercise it. The bonus is that your voice benefits from the use of your muscles. And the capacity of your voice to represent you gives you power.

Looking Ahead

I hope these stories dramatize vividly where you are headed if you stick with this program of relaxation, breathing, and voice exercises.

Developing your own sound comes first. And to experience a refreshing and energizing sound, you must first learn to free yourself from the viselike grip of tension and choked air supply. Then and only then will you be able to find your authentic voice.

With this first step, you'll begin the process of clearing obstructions from your sound, your flow of words, and the ideas they express.

The three exercises in this step—Relaxation, Breathing, and AIRobics for the Voice—make up Voice Exercise #1 (repeated in the "Voice Work" appendix). Do them daily for one week. Then, add an *additional* exercise (from the same appendix) each week in sequence until you are doing all seven voice exercises every day (or as often as you can). You can devote as much time as you wish to practice, but aim for at least 30 minutes each day. Doing all seven of the voice exercises will add up to about 30 to 45 minutes.

Enjoy the sound of your own voice!

Assignment One

1. Do your relaxation exercise, as explained on page 197.

2. Do your breathing exercise, as explained on page 198.

3. Do your vocalization exercise, AIRobics for the voice, as explained on pages 198 and 199.

SCHEDULE FOR WORKSHOP #1

(Review page 24 for more on how to start the group.)

1. Introductions

2. Go around the room and answer the "Pearly Gates" question.

3. Do Voice Exercise #1 (pages 197, 198, and 199) as a group.

4. Read through Assignment Two together (at the end of Step Two), so everyone has an idea of what will be happening at the next session.

5. *Homework:* Read Step Two and prepare to do Assignment Two at the next meeting.

▼

Get a Response and Structure Your Thoughts

1. Out of clutter, find simplicity.
2. From discord, find harmony.
*3. In the middle of difficulty lies
   opportunity.*

ALBERT EINSTEIN
"THREE RULES OF WORK"

This chapter explains two concepts that form the foundation of a successful and fearlessly given speech:

1. Get an immediate response from your audience.
2. Structure what you have to tell them with a beginning, a middle, and an end.

We'll learn some useful techniques for getting feedback from your audience with an initial response. Then we'll study a simple planned presentation with a beginning, a middle, and an end. Finally, we'll practice linking the two.

What do I mean when I ask you to get an immediate response from your audience?

A response is feedback—an indication that your listeners have received the thought you just expressed. It's an acknowledgment that they heard, understood, and are continuing to listen with interest.

There are many ways of getting a response, and we will discuss them in this chapter. You can ask a direct question, make a startling statement, tell a story, show a picture or use a prop. Your feedback can take the form of spoken answers to your question, it can be laughter, "ohs" and "ahs" or other audible responses, gestures, smiles, nods, a recognizable look of "Oh, yes! I get it!"—whatever you see or hear from the audience that says you have made a connection.

Why is getting an immediate response in this manner so critically important? Because, when you make that initial connection to your listeners, you are no longer isolated, all alone up there with only the sound of your own voice. Response creates a confidence-building bond between you and the person you're speaking to. And when you get a response from 1 person in a group of 20 people, 19 other people automatically react. You are, in a sense, speaking personally to each one. If you speak to all 20 people as a group, no one responds directly.

After you get a response you can set up the structure of your talk by determining for your listener where you are headed. Your beginning, middle, and end flow naturally from the way you seek that initial response and the kind of response you seek.

And for you, if you are a fearful speaker, making that person-to-person connection is the best way to begin to relieve your anxiety about speaking.

Think of seeking a response and establishing structure this way: It's really just a formalized version of the way you communicate informally all the time.

You have something to say. You seek your listener's attention, get a response to be sure you have that attention, and then state what you want to communicate. Like this:

"Bill, got a minute? [He nods.] This is my idea about the Jones deal . . ."

"Johnny, look at me! [He does.] Didn't I tell you not to bring your skis into the living room?"

"Tom, here's your suit from the cleaners. Tom? Tom! [He looks up from the television.] Honey, take your suit before I drop it."

All day long we communicate comfortably, fearlessly, compellingly, amusingly, even annoyingly—calling one another's attention, getting a response, and then sharing our knowledge and ideas. The process is natural, organic—until we step in front of an audience. Panicked by the sea of faces, intimidated by the need to give a formal, planned presentation, we either forget or forgo the initial connection humans require to communicate.

By continuing to get a response throughout your talk—as you'll learn in Step Three, Establish a Dialogue—you maintain your connection with your listeners.

By reaching out to the audience, you focus on what *they* need and want—namely, the story you have to tell them, the feelings and ideas you have to share. You are inviting them to come with you to a destination you have chosen, not just sit there passively. Once the journey begins, you'll be surprised and delighted at how your fear will fade.

Eight Ways to Get a Response

1. Ask a Direct Question to One Member of the Audience

This powerful technique is especially effective for those who have fear of speaking. That's why I emphasize it so strongly in this program and encourage you to use it. To repeat, asking a direct question to one person establishes an immediate connection between you and your listeners. When you get an immediate response from one person, every other person in the room responds. When you talk to one, you are talking to all. The focus is off of you. It is on the subject. The audience is aroused. You are not isolated or afraid.

Consider the difference between this opening:

> Millions of immigrants entered the United States through Ellis Island during its long history. They came from every corner of the world, and found their way to every state in the union . . .

And this opening:

> Sam, do you have parents, or grandparents, or great-grandparents, who entered the United States through Ellis Island?

If he says, "Yes," pursue it further. "Grandparents? Well so do I."

If he says, "No, my family goes back to the *Mayflower*," you can talk about that, or ask if anyone else has relatives who came to the United States through Ellis Island.

The first version is accurate enough and promises an informative speech. But it's dry in tone and sets up the speaker as an impersonal narrator—an initial impression that will be difficult to overcome.

The second, however, establishes a bond between speaker and audience. We are a nation of immigrants; everyone's forebears came from somewhere. That's why a visit to Ellis Island is such a moving experience, even for those who trace their lineage all the way back to the *Mayflower*.

2. Make a Startling Statement or Ask a Provocative Question

If you were listening to a talk on volcanoes, which opening would grab your attention? If you were giving the talk, which would be most comfortable for you? This:

> Volcanic activity is as old as the earth and continues to this day. In our own time, Mt. St. Helens covered a vast region of the state of Washington with lava and ash. And scientists expect Mt. Vesuvius, the volcano that buried the ancient Roman city of Pompeii, to erupt again.

Or this:

> Anna, did you know Mt. Vesuvius is expected to erupt again? The ancient volcano that destroyed the Roman city of Pompeii is expected to erupt again and do the same to the city of Milan.

Anna might respond, "Hmmm. That may change my vacation plans to go to Italy next summer," and here you have a give-and-take going. But you are in control, and you can bridge to your main points. "Today I'm going to talk about . . ."

3. Describe a Shared Experience

Identifying a shared experience connects speaker and audience. For example:

> Where were you, James, when that big nor'easter hit last winter? . . . How about you, Gladys? . . . Well, I was literally in the clouds that produced all that snow. I was stuck in an office on the 100th floor of the Empire State Building . . .

The device is handy in business presentations, too:

I know you share my feeling, George, and Lisa, and all of you, that we are setting the standard in this industry. That's why what I have to share with you today is so exciting . . .

4. Give the Latest News

Lou Gerstner, CEO of IBM Corporation, began a speech to his company's shareholders with this plainly stated but tantalizing news bulletin:

> I'd like to start with some news of interest to all of you here. This morning your board of directors approved a 10 percent increase in the quarterly dividend—from 20 to 22 cents per common share. Of course, that's on a post-split basis. This means that over the past three years, your dividend payments have increased by 76 percent. The dividend is payable on June 10 to shareholders of record May 8.

Gerstner got everyone's attention instantly with this flash. He knew that because his announcement was greeted with enthusiastic applause; he had sought and received a response from his listeners.

Following this exchange, the shareholders were in a friendly and eager state of mind. They settled back to listen to everything else their company's top officer had to tell them about the status of their investment.

5. Ask Your Audience to Do Something

Call for a show of hands. Ask everyone to stand up and stretch. Turn around and introduce yourself to your seatmates.

Psychotherapist and author Jerilyn Ross has her own unique way of connecting to an audience. She begins a speech describing panic disorder by asking each person to close his or her eyes:

> Imagine that you are crossing a street with your two-year-old child (or your grandchild, niece, or nephew). You are holding the child's hand when suddenly a car comes speeding toward you. You grip the child's hand tightly and try to get out of the way of the car. But as you're running across the street you don't feel the child's hand anymore. It has slipped away.

Now, with your eyes still closed, imagine your reaction at that moment when the hand slipped away—your heart's pounding, you feel light-headed, disoriented, and a sense of impending doom and stark terror. That's a normal, healthy reaction to losing a child in the middle of oncoming traffic.

Now imagine that you're standing on line about to buy groceries, sitting watching a movie in a theater, or giving a speech. Suddenly, for no apparent reason, you feel the same intensity of fear and panic. There's no threat of danger, no child about to be hurt. Not only do you feel the horrible physiological feelings but also the sense of "Oh my God, what's wrong with me? I seem to be going crazy."

That's what happens to people who suffer from panic disorder.

Jerilyn Ross's technique of starting a speech does two things: (1) It helps her connect to her audience, and (2) it establishes a frame of reference for the rest of her speech. It works and makes the point powerfully. Every person in the audience can relate to the feelings of real panic and get a sense of what it might be like for a person who has panic disorder.

6. Relate an Anecdote or Tell a Joke

Anecdotes, jokes, and riddles are effective response-getters if—and I want to emphasize this—and only if they are genuinely funny, appropriate for the audience, and pertinent to the topic you are going to discuss.

For now, I advise you not to get hung up on them. If you can share a funny story with your audience—especially one in which they might be involved—good. But don't spend a lot of time searching joke books and anthologies of quotations looking for instant wit. Fearless speaking is an exploration of substance that comes from the heart and is motivated by conviction, not a mastery of stand-up comedy. The notion that every good speech *must* begin with a snappy joke is deeply ingrained in our expectations, however, and it's hard to get people to abandon it.

I worked with a Fortune 500 company that was so wedded to the idea that executives who gave speeches were *required* to begin with a joke. To help them, the company compiled a computerized joke bank. Funny stories were filed by category.

Executives preparing speeches could access jokes that seemed to be related to their subjects. The computer file would tell the joke's entire history—who used it, when, and where. Based on this information, an executive could decide if this was the joke that was needed and wanted, and if it was fresh enough.

For certain speakers and certain occasions, a file like this would be a handy tool. But it's not for everyone all the time. Making the inclusion of a joke mandatory can give the moment a canned quality that gets the speech off to a shaky start—exactly the opposite of the desired effect.

William S. Paley, CEO of CBS, was deft at including humor in his speeches. Nine times out of ten, however, he would veto anecdotes or jokes his speechwriters suggested because he didn't feel the material reflected his natural humor. He had impeccable taste, clarity of thought, and an honest sense of himself. With him, less was more.

7. Give a Demonstration; Use Props

The same is true of demonstrations and the use of props. If you can show as well as tell, you will have everyone's undivided attention immediately. If your line is raincoats, for instance, this might fill the bill.

Depending on the size of your audience, you might ask one person to come forward and model the products you're promoting:

> Geraldine, come up here, please, and try on this raincoat. We're here today to look at our new wrinkle-proof raincoat, and I know we're all very excited about this revolutionary product. How wrinkle-proof is it? Well, just look at this. These two raincoats spent the night stuffed in a bag. Here's our competitor's [pulls a disheveled coat out of the bag]. Looks like somebody slept in it, doesn't it? Now, here's ours, wrinkle-proofed with our brand new process, Eversmooth [the second coat is crisp and wrinkle-free]. A difference we can be proud of, don't you think?"

8. Ask a Barrage of Questions; Use Slides

For example:

> Jerry, have you been to the Rock and Roll Hall of Fame? Jacobs Field? The Flats? Downtown Cleveland is truly the Miracle on Lake

Erie, isn't it? [Show slide of downtown Cleveland, alive with light and color and movement.] It's hard to imagine it any other way. But here's Cleveland not so long ago. [Show slide of dingy, deserted downtown streets.] In those days, you may recall, they were calling it the "Big Mistake on the Lake." A renaissance seemed impossible then . . .

Whatever you choose, make sure you get an immediate response from one person in the audience, and everyone else will respond. Enjoy the feeling that goes with knowing they want to hear more. This takes the focus off of you and your fear.

A Response-Getter's Tools

1. Ask a question.
2. Be provocative.
3. Share an experience.
4. Give the latest news.
5. Ask the audience to do something.
6. Tell an anecdote, a joke, or a riddle.
7. Give a demonstration; use props.
8. Ask a barrage of questions; use slides.

STRUCTURE

1. *Beginning*
   Get a response.
   Tell them what you're going to tell them.
2. *Middle*
   State your major points.
   Elaborate, explain, illustrate each.
   Tell them.
3. *End*
   Cement and summarize what you just said.
   Tell them what you told them.

Structuring Your Thoughts

Okay, you have your audience's attention. You've invited and received a response, made a human connection, established rapport. They're with you.

Now, where do you take them?

Your presentation needs a beginning, a middle, and an end. This simple outline is your best defense against fear of speaking. Why? Because by filling in this three-step outline with your expertise, insight, knowledge, and understanding, you yourself will be filled with the exhilaration and the enthusiasm that comes with sharing your special interest in a subject. When you're excited about a subject, your inner fire ignites the person you're speaking to, and it kindles chemistry between the two of you. All of this begins with the process of structuring your presentation.

You may be called on to make off-the-cuff remarks during a discussion or a meeting, but even these should be thoughtful and worthwhile expressions of your knowledge and experience. Your listeners need facts, figures, and truths from you. To make a presentation by winging it may not merit the attention of your audience. Nor would a speech that has not been thought out logically or that doesn't use any of the aforementioned eight ways to get a response. It's as if you invited people to your home, opened the door, greeted them, then left them to their own devices by not engaging them or keeping them entertained and involved.

Planning Your Remarks: Start in the Middle

You know that getting a response is the first thing you do when you get up to speak. But in your preparation, the first thing you need to do is plan what you're going to say. The response-getter you choose is the transition into the structure of your remarks.

Look at the preceding box. Which part of the presentation is the meat of your talk, the nitty-gritty, the very reason you've come before this audience? The middle, of course.

Begin your preparation by listing your major points. Use facts and statistics to support their significance. Think of several examples to illustrate each point. If an anecdote or funny story comes to mind that might illuminate one of your points, jot it down in the outline, too.

When you're finished, you'll have the plot of your talk laid out from start to finish. Then wrapping it up is easy: Just summarize what you've said, and perhaps leave them with a memorable quote or anecdote.

Then, think about your opening. With the heart and soul of what you have to say firmly in place—and even some of the words you will use running through your mind already—choosing an appropriate opening will be easier.

That's because you are now thinking of your opening, your response-getter, in the right way. Now your opening is a greeting, a salutation, an invitation, a door through which you and your listeners walk together. It's not a separate performance element, to be executed with a flourish merely for its own sake.

Your Turn

Let's start in a low-key, nonthreatening manner—with a planned presentation to just one person instead of to an audience.

Begin by choosing a friend, family member, or coworker. Select a subject that is near and dear to you. Something you know well. Something you believe will give pleasure and enlightenment to your listener and perhaps even improve his or her life.

Begin by listing your main points:

- What do you want your listener to take away from this presentation?
- What facts can you share from your own research?
- What can you tell him or her that is unique from your experience and understanding?

If your objective is to prove that a vegetarian diet is more healthful than a diet including meat, for example:

MIDDLE

Main points:

- My cholesterol went up to 284. I became a vegetarian, and here's what I eat.

- Why I gave up eating meat.
- How long it takes to digest animal fat compared to vegetables and fruit. Why and how body chemistry affects the digestion of food.
- The benefits of being a vegetarian and how I:
  lost weight
  have more energy
  lowered my cholesterol
- The problems I've had being a vegetarian and how I've overcome them: how I order in a restaurant, get enough protein, keep my diet interesting.

END

Summary: Vegetarianism in philosophy and practice, and why I chose it as my lifestyle.

Now, think about how you want to begin your presentation. How you want to Get a Response from your listener.

Following are some possibilities, based on the techniques we studied earlier in this chapter.

BEGINNING

Tom, are you concerned about improving your diet? . . . I am, too. Let me take you to a restaurant that specializes in vegetarian food. I'd like to tell you what I've done with my diet, and why.

Or:

Susan, have you ever had a veggie burger? Well, here is your first. It's every bit as tasty today as a hamburger, but it's much healthier. Let me tell you why.

Or:

You mentioned that you're concerned because your daughter has stopped eating meat. Is that so? Well, don't worry. I gave up meat, too, and I have found that . . .

Here's another example of how an effective speech is outlined by beginning, middle, and end. This time I'm reprinting it for you in its finished sequence—beginning, middle, end.

WENDY'S STORY
How Alcoholics Anonymous Helped Me

During what she describes as the "boozy blur" of her 20s, Wendy had many jobs and lived many places.

By the time she came to class, Wendy, then in her early 30s, was sober, back in school, and well on her way to a degree in social work. Her fear of speaking at Alcoholics Anonymous meetings, in class, and everywhere else stemmed from feelings of inadequacy: She felt that she had nothing interesting to share. These feelings led to panic, and then to avoidance.

The Seven Steps to Fearless Speaking Program showed her that she has plenty to say, insights to share, and valuable experience others can learn from. She made the talk at AA that she had been dreading, and one night in class, Wendy celebrated her newfound sense of freedom with this well-organized talk about her experience at AA.

BEGINNING

Response-getter:

> On the first day of class, Lilyan asked us why we took this course. I wanted to say, but was too frightened, "I would like to be able to speak at Alcoholics Anonymous, at my seventh anniversary meeting this year. As of this Friday, I will have been sober for seven years."

What she's going to tell them:

> The 12-step program of AA worked for me. It has helped many addicts. It can help you, too.

MIDDLE

   I. Outside help
      A. Often is required.
      B. Someone is always available.

  II. The people in the program
      A. Understand your misery.
      B. Everyone is there for the same reason.

 III. How I got to AA
      A. Seven years ago I fell when I was drunk.
      B. Hit my head and almost died.

C. Went to a detoxification program, mandatory AA.

D. Attended 90 meetings in 90 days.

END

I am here today as living proof that the program works. I haven't had a drink in seven years. I didn't drink today, and I know I will make the same decision tomorrow. This 12-step program can work for you, too.

You can do that. . . . You can:

get a response immediately,

tell them what I'm going to tell them,

tell them, and

tell them what you told them

. . . but will it stop your panic, shaking hands, sick feeling? Try it. But don't use any shortcuts. Have an outline that is clear and easy to see. Practice it out loud. Set a time schedule for yourself. Then *do* it.

PAUL'S COMPELLING EXAMPLE OF FEARLESS SPEAKING
Savor the Juice of the Grape

Paul, an accountant, gave a one-on-one presentation that is a model for this exercise. Simple, to the point, developed from his own deep interests, Paul's talk demonstrates vividly the lessons of this chapter: how to Get a Response and Structure Your Thoughts.

Paul's passion is wine. He loves studying, collecting, and enjoying fine wine. His desire for knowledge is so great, he took a wine course at Windows on the World at New York City's World Trade Center. Then he couldn't wait to share what he learned.

But Paul is a perfectionist and imagined that he had to write out his presentation word for word before he could give it. Otherwise, he insisted, he would panic and forget what he wanted to say.

Paul began to overcome these fears by giving his wine talk, from notes instead of from a full text, to just one person in a relaxed, informal setting. He found a friend who also loved wine, but hadn't had the benefit of Paul's training, and invited the friend to dinner at a restaurant with an extensive wine list.

Following the middle-first approach, Paul planned to use the selection of a red wine to go with dinner as a framework for explaining to his friend the meaning of body, color, and tannin in wine; the varieties of red wine available; and where each comes from.

At the end he planned to summarize the lesson, review the wines available to them, and ask the friend to help him make a choice.

His opening, then, practically wrote itself: "Do you enjoy red wine? Do the choices in red wine confuse you?" Predictably, the friend admitted always being confused.

Here, then, is an approximation of how Paul's one-on-one presentation played out. He used an outline. But with each student, I record the speech as it's given. So here is the scenario as Paul recorded it.

BEGINNING

Paul gets a response:

> PAUL: Do you enjoy red wine? What's your favorite grape? Do the choices in red wine confuse you?
>
> FRIEND: Yes, I love red wine, but I never know what to choose.
>
> PAUL: I used to feel that way, too. Then last summer I took the wine course at Windows on the World. It improved my understanding and my enjoyment of wine immensely. If you like, I'd love to tell you about body, color, tannin, and alternatives to American pinot noirs, merlots, and cabernets. Then you can choose the wine for dinner from the wine list.
>
> FRIEND: Great!

MIDDLE

Paul explains the varieties of red wine:

> PAUL: First let's decide what we're having for dinner. Filet mignon? Good choice. I'll have that, too. Now, let's go through this wine list and identify the varieties of red grapes represented here. I see that they are listed in gradations of body, color, and tannin.
>
> FRIEND: What does that mean?
>
> PAUL: I'll tell you. Let's start with body. Light body is like skim milk. Full body is like whole milk. Lighter wines are easier to

drink with no food or light foods. One way to tell a wine body is by color. The lighter-body wines like pinot noir are lighter in color than a full-bodied cabernet. A merlot is somewhere in between.

FRIEND: What's tannin?

PAUL: Tannin comes from the skins, stems, and pits of the grape all floating around in the tank. If the wine is aged in oak—and these were—the wine picks up tannin. It's not really a taste, it's a sensation. It's the dry mouth feeling you get after tasting wine. First you taste the fruit. It may be a little acidic. Then 30 to 60 seconds later, you get the flavor of tannin. Tannin is strongest in a full-bodied wine like cabernet. I hope this isn't getting too confusing.

FRIEND: No, I'm not confused. I'm eager to select.

END

Choosing the wine:

PAUL: Good. Let me review. Any one of the wines listed here—the pinot noir, merlot, or cabernet sauvignon—is good with red meat. We could order pinot noir because it is lighter in body and color. Or the cabernet, which is full-bodied, darker, and has more tannin. Or the merlot, which is medium in body and color. Which shall it be? Shall we ask for a sample of each? What happens if we like them all?

FRIEND: All I can say is—Cheers!

Paul and his friend proceeded to have dinner beginning with a merlot wine.

Remember, you are *not* just having a conversation with a friend. Although your friend may interrupt, react, or ask questions, your job is to stay on track. Get a response. Structure your thoughts. Proceed through your main points. Then, summarize what you've said, and receive your friend's appreciation.

And—best of all—enjoy your first taste of fearless speaking.

In this step, you've learned how to seek response and build structure. These two actions are the foundation of fearless, successful speaking. Thinking ahead, Step Three presents a further challenge—

learning how to dialogue. Keeping in mind what really matters to you, as you continue with the Seven Step Program, you will explore the areas of life you know best and want to share with colleagues at work, with family, and with friends. Dialogue, creativity, persuasion, objective, and conviction are the next great mountains to climb.

Assignment Two

Give a five- to eight-minute presentation to one person, getting a response at the start, and structuring your talk with a beginning, a middle, and an end.

1. Choose as a topic something you know about and can explain.

2. Choose your audience of one—a friend, coworker, relative, spouse, partner.

3. Choose the place of the presentation—over lunch or dinner, in your living room or office.

4. Decide how you will get a response from your listener. Choose from the devices described earlier in this chapter, or make up one of your own.

5. Structure and outline your remarks, beginning with the middle of the presentation. List your major points and your supporting material for each. As an ending, summarize them. Then, plan your beginning.

6. Think through your presentation. Make a list of the major points so you can repeat them in your mind from memory.

7. Keep your written outline in front of you as you practice the presentation aloud.

8. Record your presentation. Play it back. Is it clear? Is your response-getter provocative? Is what you are saying important to you?

9. You're on! Go out and give the speech for real. Record it.

10. Listen to the tape and answer the questions in the Self-Critique Questionnaire for Step Two.

11. Turn to page 197 in Appendix A. Begin practicing with Voice Exercise #1, then add Voice Exercise #2. Continue to practice exercises in sequence every day.

Self-Critique Questionnaire for Step Two

▶ Did I cover all the points I planned to cover? If I left out a point, was it crucial to the talk? Or am I being perfectionistic?

▶ Did I get a response right away? What was it? Was it the response I wanted? Did it bring the person I was speaking to closer to me?

▶ Did I get additional responses I hadn't counted on? Did I allow responses to become too lengthy, or did I cut them off by rushing to my next point?

▶ Was it fun? Why?

SCHEDULE FOR WORKSHOP #2

1. Do Voice Exercises #1 and #2 (in the "Voice Work" appendix) as a group. (And from now on you'll do them daily by yourself, as well.)

2. Choose a partner and give your prepared one-on-one speech to him or her. (Take turns until everyone has given his or her speech.)

3. After everyone has finished, take a few minutes and answer your Self-Critique Questionnaire for Step Two, and share your answers with the group. This is the time to discuss how you think you did and how it felt to you. Try to get some constructive criticism from the group.

4. Read through Assignment Three (for next time) together.

5. *Homework:* Read Step Three and prepare to do Assignment Three at the next meeting.

Establish a Dialogue

*I have always believed that a lot of
the problems in the world would
disappear if people would start talking to each other instead of talking
about each other.*

RONALD REAGAN

All over the country, right now, thousands of people are standing up in boardrooms, facing PTA audiences, giving opening remarks at charity banquets, or making wedding toasts.

But, although thousands of people are giving public speeches, very few are communicating. Instead, they are reading aloud words they, or a speechwriter, put together on paper. These are serious, important pieces of information. And the audiences are dutifully playing their part—trying to listen, pretending to take notes, clapping politely at the finish.

Yet, once in a while, the scenario comes alive. It acquires a freshness, a sense of spontaneity. The speaker is totally engaging. He seems to be talking *personally* to everyone in the room! The audience finds real pleasure in the presentation and takes away something to think about, and even savor, for a long time.

What's the difference?

The speaker in the second scenario has engaged the audience by establishing a dialogue.

What, exactly, does this mean? Why is dialogue necessary? And how will it help you to become a fearless speaker? These are the questions I'll answer in this chapter.

I know from experience that what I am going to tell you may be difficult to believe at first. The idea of establishing a dialogue with your listeners seems revolutionary to many people; it's contrary to the way they've been conditioned to think about public speaking.

One of the major goals of this Seven Step Program, however, is to show you what will happen to your fear when you abandon talking *at* your audience and begin speaking *with* them.

Like getting a response, opening a dialogue is not just a mechanical technique. ("I'm three minutes into my speech. It's time to ask a question.") It's finding a way to establish a *sustained* human connection with your listeners, a give-and-take that is based on substance, not on speaking devices: on what you have to say and your audience's response to it.

Within a speech, dialogue can take several different forms. The simplest is a direct exchange with a small group, in which you, the speaker, address individuals in the audience and invite responses from them on a regular basis during your talk. It is more difficult to get dialogue going with an auditorium full of people. With a group of 50 or more, it is not necessary to get actual comments, but laughter, applause, nods, smiles of recognition, looks of concern, approval, and even disagreement are forms of communication. Expressions like these tell you that your listeners are with you.

Example: At a luncheon honoring 12 doctors and scientists researching the cure for breast cancer, Evelyn Lauder, founder of the Breast Cancer Research Foundation and a top executive at Estée Lauder Companies, structured her speech to get a dialogue going.

Five years ago at the Pierre Hotel there were 200 attendees at our symposium and luncheon. Today we needed the Waldorf Astoria to accommodate 800 of you. [Applause.] This is a great testament to the strides being made in the field of breast cancer research and to the distinguished panel of researchers. We learned a great deal at our panel this morning. We learned about estrogen, breast health, and about diet as well. For those of you who missed our symposium this morning, this is our way of giving back information to you so that you know where your money has gone. I'm thrilled to announce that we are awarding $4 million in grants for research this year. [More applause.] We are also deeply grateful to Ms. Estée Lauder for underwriting this luncheon. Special thanks to my four co-chairs. [Bigger applause.] And thanks to you, today's luncheon has netted over $1 million. [Biggest applause.]

Amid the clatter of silverware and dishes, Evelyn Lauder's voice rang out clearly and forcefully as she began her remarks. She built fact upon fact to get a response in the form of applause to involve and dialogue with the audience.

Reach out to your audience for a connection.

Imagine you are speaking to a group. You make an initial connection—get a response. Then you state the purpose of your talk and begin going through your points. But what if you feel yourself fading into the woodwork? What if you begin to lose your train of thought as you look out at faces beginning to show a loss of interest or connection?

As you feel your audience drifting away, reacting just as you would if you were in their seats and the speaker "went flat," your confidence begins to crumble. A down-spiral toward panic is under way.

What happened? You got an initial response, but you didn't *keep additional responses coming*. That's what dialogue is all about: *sustaining* your initial connection to your listeners, refreshing it, enlivening it. It's about reaching out throughout your speech, carrying your listeners with you on a delightful, informative journey you have so carefully mapped out for them.

Remember, getting a response is much more than just a way of breaking the ice. Fearless speaking comes from sincere, person-to-person contact. Consequently, if you treat your response-getter as a gimmick and then abandon it, reverting to the "same old same old," you'll suffer the same old consequence of debilitating fear.

Getting a response means targeting a person and stimulating a thought or action in that person. Once that thought or action is acknowledged, you move on to another person. Establishing a dialogue means keeping that give-and-take going for as long or short a period as you choose—depending on the nature of your speech.

In tennis, for example, you keep the ball in action until a point is made. The same holds true for speaking. You keep the train of thought going until you've made and clinched your point. Then, as in tennis, you start the action again—with another serve, keep the give-and-take going—until the game is won or you have fulfilled the objective of your speech.

"Let the Church Say 'Amen!' "

For good examples of the importance of establishing a dialogue, we need look no further than our houses of worship.

Clergy who have to face and attempt to motivate their flocks every Saturday or Sunday are intimately familiar with the need to establish dialogue—and with what happens when they don't. (Parishioners, too, know the difference: When do you listen, and when do your thoughts wander to dinner or the afternoon's yard work?)

Without a sustained connection between pulpit and pew, religious observance, which is built around highly scripted ritual to begin with, quickly becomes mechanistic and dry.

One of the most important reforms undergone by the Catholic Church as a result of Vatican II was the decision to have the priest face the congregation during celebration of the Eucharist. The old way—facing the altar with his back to the congregation—wasn't conducive to a true feeling of communion. Nor was the tradition of conducting the Mass in Latin, an ancient language spoken only by priests. These changes made an enormous difference to the feeling of involvement and the interest of the members of the Catholic congregation.

Another way churches and synagogues try to include their congregations is through responsorials—portions of the service spoken or sung by the congregation in dialogue with the minister or rabbi.

Evangelists like the Reverend Billy Graham, who routinely preach to tens of thousands in giant arenas, hold their audiences rapt by making their messages highly personal and seeking frequent responses.

In Orthodox Jewish synagogues, the cantor leads the prayers. The congregation rises and sits at certain sections of the prayers. While standing, some sway back and forth. This is a personal preference. There are responsive readings as well during the service. Dialoguing like this between the cantor and the congregation is reverent as well as exuberant.

And in African-American churches, where ebullient worship is often the norm, preachers don't hesitate to ask for the response they want: They say, "Let the church say 'Amen!' "

These forms of prayer foster feelings of belonging—of being included, responsive, and involved in worship. That is the objective of dialoguing: inclusion, involvement, and response.

Breaking Down the Fourth Wall

In the theater, an invisible fourth wall is imagined between the stage and the audience. The characters in the play enact their life drama as if oblivious to the audience that is watching their every move and listening to their every word.

In reality, of course, the actors on the stage are keenly sensitive to the response they are getting from the theatergoers out there in the dark. But the convention of pretending the audience doesn't exist, and never stepping out of character by acknowledging the audience, is necessary in purely representational drama.

What fun it is, however, to attend a play that is purely presentational in style and format—in which a narrator, or perhaps all the characters, talk directly to us. In Terrence McNally's *Master Class*, for example, Maria Callas treats the audience as if it were her students. In *Our Town*, the narrator talks directly to the audience. Plays like these are almost always crowd pleasers. We love to feel connected to what's happening on stage. I remember being in the audience at a performance of *Master Class*, raising my hand vigorously, in answer to a direct question, wanting to be included in the action. Even though I was passed over, I felt I was included because I was encouraged to respond. Skillful actors spark and maintain that sense of interaction, making us feel as if we are part of the action, in on the jokes, hip to the spirit of the proceedings.

So reach out and touch your audience. When you do that as a speaker, your fear is replaced by the joy of real communication.

You Dialogue Daily

I can hear you say, "Bully for preachers and actors. But what they do is pretty exotic compared to what *I* have to do—namely, explain to our marketing department why the shoes we make are going to have rounder toes next year, why our pants will be baggier, and why our dominant colors will be beige and burnt orange. How do I make them say 'Amen!' to that, without my voice quivering and my knees knocking?"

Well, you can.

You already know how to dialogue. You do it all the time. If the techniques of the pulpit and the stage seem too far-fetched, consider what you do in your daily life.

When you really want to communicate, you do not take communication for granted. You do not assume that what you're saying is being understood. You make sure it's understood. For example, you're rushing out the door to work or school. You have only two minutes to make the train, or avoid traffic, but there's one more thing to communicate before you leave.

"Susan, I just remembered, you must pick up your dress at the cleaners by 5 or you won't have it for tomorrow's trip. Susan, did you hear that? You know what cleaners I'm talking about? They're on Peartree Avenue by the mall. Peartree *Avenue,* not Street. Got it?"

Or at the office, because you're sure that the other person's secretary never gives your messages the attention they deserve:

"Ms. Marsh, could you make sure this envelope gets to Marv Hendricks by noon? I've marked it 'urgent' right here in the corner. I'd appreciate it if you'd let me know when he's received it. Could you give me a call?"

All day long we probe our listeners for a sign of understanding. We stir up their thoughts with provocative statements. We ask for the acknowledgment we want. And we seek more than an initial response. We seek a constant interchange of information.

That's what you need to do in your talks. Here's how.

How to Plan Dialogue

In Step Two, you learned and practiced several methods of getting an initial response from your listeners: asking a question, making a provocative statement, telling a funny or touching story, showing an object that illustrates your presentation.

You can continue to use any and all of these to stay in touch with your listeners.

Depending on the size of the group and the venue, your dialogue can be a literal dialogue or an implied one. You can invite interruptions and questions as you go through your presentation. Allow time and space for less-audible audience reaction.

How often should you seek an additional response? There's no formula. You need to stay on top of the situation. Don't wait until their attention disappears. Keep feeding them stimuli, so there is never a dull moment.

Be a sleuth. Focus on the vibes you're getting from the audience. If you're not getting any, you may be in trouble. If you find yourself talking for seven or eight minutes without getting a response, you *are* in trouble. Ten minutes, and you've probably lost most of them.

So what do you do every five or six minutes to keep your audience connected with you?

Here are some commonly used devices to get you started. They can be used alone or in combination. Use them all in the same talk if they fit. My only hard-and-fast rule is this: Keep the audience reacting.

1. Ask Direct Questions

The response-getter most favored by my students is a direct question: "Did you ever . . ." "Can you imagine . . ." "What do you think would happen if . . ." It's highly effective when speaking to small groups because you can address audience members directly and they can answer.

If the group is larger, ask the questions of everyone, and look and listen for responses—nods, smiles of recognition, "uh-huhs."

And don't worry—if you've structured your talk well, you won't get off track. If responses make you lose your train of thought, you can always refer to your outline.

2. Ask Rhetorical Questions

In effect, conduct your own Q&A. Introduce each new segment of your presentation with a question: "Why is this so important . . . ? Let me tell you . . ." "What will happen if we don't . . . ? Here's what will happen . . ." "Does this traditional approach make sense in our high-tech world . . . ? You bet it does . . ."

This method of dialoguing is a logical reflection of the structure of your talk and is particularly effective when your objective is to be persuasive.

3. Tell a Story

An anecdote, especially a personal one, reinforces the rapport you carefully established at the beginning of your talk. If appropriate, preface your story with something like this: "Here's an example of what I mean, and it really happened to me . . ." or "What I'm saying here really struck home for me when . . ." An anecdote, particularly a humorous or touching one, brings you down off the podium in the minds of the listeners and reconnects you with them on a person-to-person basis. One of my students accidentally dropped her dorm keys into a bag belonging to a young man she was interested in, but who she knew had another girlfriend. Was her face red when she found the keys! But she kept our attention while telling this story, which helped to make her point—that unisex articles, particularly backpacks, can be dangerous.

4. Act Out Portions of Your Story

Conditioned by years of television comedy and sitcom, we all love to act out the funny and exciting moments of our lives—how we outsmarted some salesperson or shut down the boss's bossy secretary or what happened when *he* popped the question or *she* accepted. You'll get a laugh, win friends, and sustain your dialogue. And later, you'll wonder where your fear went.

5. Bring Something to Show

Visual aids enhance any presentation. But do you know why? Because they are dialoguing devices. Not only do they illustrate what you're saying, they help get and keep your audience's attention.

Except for this: Slides can be sleep inducing when they are not stimulating. When the lights are turned down, people tend to doze. It becomes more necessary than ever to structure and dramatize your presentation. If they are good slides—interesting, vivid attention-grabbers containing pictures of what you are talking about, not portions of your text in large letters—slides can be potent dialoguing devices.

6. Wave Flags, Give Orders—Nicely

As the speaker, you are, by definition, the expert here. So if you say, "What will happen to the market as a result . . . and this is important to understand . . . ," they will listen to you and renew their attention.

Giving orders and directions works, too. Like this: "There are three ways to do this. If you have a pencil, I recommend writing them down." Or "Don't worry, help is available. There's a toll-free number for tech support. Here it is [on a chart, or you write it on a blackboard]. You may want to jot this down."

7. Handouts

If at all possible, distribute something. A brochure, a leaflet, a news release, or even an entire press kit complete with photocopied articles and photographs—all these are top-notch handouts. But take this precaution. Sometimes people get so engrossed in the handouts, they don't listen. Or they fiddle with them, which distracts them and you.

Something as simple as a one-page digest of information—a tip sheet, a list of dos and don'ts, a compilation of e-mail addresses or phone numbers—will demonstrate your preparedness to your listeners and provide you with what could be a handy dialoguing device at the same time.

A word of caution: *Decide carefully when you want the handouts to be in people's hands. If it's during your speech, you may lose the audience's attention. Aim it toward a time when you and the audience can examine the handout together.*

8. Get Physical, with Caution

Asking your audience to do something physical—to get up, shake hands with the people around them, touch their toes, stand on one foot—can be fun for you and for them. But be careful. Know who you are talking to, and think carefully about what, exactly, you want them to do.

Some people absolutely hate audience participation. They avoid folk music because they don't want to sing along. A theater critic I know was enraged when he was required, as part of a performance of a Broadway show, to stand up and do the hokey-pokey.

So use good taste and show graciousness. You'll win more friends that way.

9. Pause Strategically

Depending on how you've structured your talk, you can pause at strategic intervals. In a large auditorium, it's a chance to collect everyone's ear. In a small venue, it's an opportunity for comment. Also, pauses give the audience a chance to digest what you've said. And pausing invites response. Even if it's only a mental response, it reminds listeners to actively consider what you are saying.

10. Be a Sleuth

Watch and listen during your presentation. Look at the audience. Listen to them. How are they reacting? Are they getting it? Are they looking at you respectfully, adoringly, with obvious enjoyment? Are they looking at you at all? It's a good idea to tell the audience what they are communicating to you as you speak, whether it be a stony silence, enthusiastic nodding, or whatever.

The way to do this, to maintain your dialogue, is to say things like this: "You seem to disagree, Sally, why is that?" or "Jim, I noticed that you smiled broadly—did this information surprise you?" or, in the worst-case scenario, "You all seem very quiet—What information can I give you that will put us all on the same wavelength?"

If you were in a natural dialogue with only one other person present, you would notice, and respond to, the other person's body language and make that a part of your conversation. The same kind of sensory acuity can help you when you are making a speech. In fact, if you choose to ignore what the audience is communicating to you, it will create even more tension for you as the speaker. It would be like trying to hum a tune while others around the dinner table are having a conversation—the two activities would not be connected in any way.

With a little practice, you can tune in to your audience, stay tuned in, and keep them with you all the way.

Using all or some of these devices and all the energy you expend on dialoguing is worth it. You get stimulated and excited. You transfer that excitement to your audience. The audience gives back to you. There is no fear. There is exhilaration and involvement.

Who's Listening?

In Step Two, we examined the importance of knowing who your audience is—whom you're talking to—before you can know what action, if any, you want them to take.

The same holds true for Step Three. You can't establish a dialogue with them, either, unless you have at least some idea of who's listening. The more you know about your listeners, the more effective—and less fearful—you will be.

Researching your audience is a given by now, a standard and essential aspect of your preparation. If you are raising money for public television, for instance, your request is more likely to strike home if you know and acknowledge the interests and educational level of your listeners—information the station will be only too happy to provide.

If you are speaking to a group of golfers, you know they will understand how good it feels to chip a ball onto the green and watch it roll inexorably to the pin—and drop in! But if there are no golfers in the house, you are going to have to choose another metaphor.

If there isn't time or opportunity to obtain specific information about an audience, try to determine where the people come from and why they are here listening to you. The kinds of questions you might ask the program coordinator are as follows: Is attendance here voluntary or mandatory? Do these people share a common concern, such as the future of the department they work in, adherence to a new company policy, or recent changes in tax law? A common enthusiasm, such as opera, automobiles, or gardening?

If the group is small, chances are very good that you know at least some of them by name. If not, take the neighborly but usually overlooked step of simply introducing yourself and asking their names beforehand.

Another question to ask: At what time is this meeting taking place?

7:00 A.M.	(sleepy time)
11:00 A.M.	(before lunchtime)
5:00 P.M.	(rush-hour traffic time)
7:00 P.M.	(after a drink time)
9:00 P.M.	(after dinner—full meal time)

All of these times make a difference.

Never make assumptions about who's listening. Age range, gender, and race are obvious, but if you don't dig deeper, you run the risk of misperceiving your audience completely. You can't tell by looking at people

What they think

What they've read

Where they've been

What is important to them

Beyond the obvious clues to identity, respect your listeners as you want to be respected yourself. Each is a unique individual, like you. Don't talk down or up. Talk *to* them, from the heart.

Pam, an official for an international organization that works for human rights, was making herself ill worrying about a speech she had to give explaining her organization's work. When she first came to class, she was so overcome by panic, she shook through her first speech. I told her it was okay to deliver her speech sitting down. That helped. But from then on, she stood. With every speech she became more involved, and as she used the Seven Steps, the shakes diminished.

But what made the biggest difference for her—what helped her experience her first taste of less fearful, if not entirely fearless, speaking—was her continuous strong effort to *dialogue* with the class. Here's her fourth speech, in her words (and it was given standing before the class, taking control).

PAM'S COMPELLING EXAMPLE OF FEARLESS SPEAKING
The Tibetan Monk

BEGINNING

In my first talk to you three weeks ago, I suggested that you see *Kundun*, Martin Scorsese's new film about Tibet and the Dalai Lama. Who did that? Jennifer? Tell me your reaction. [Jennifer responds.] I agree. That scene stayed with me, too.

Tonight I want to give you some insight into my job and why it is so important to me. The best way for me to do this is to share with you the story of one man. Someone whom I deeply respect, and someone who is a friend. I'm going to pass around his picture.

MIDDLE

His name is Palden Gyatso. He's a Tibetan monk who, at age 65, has spent 33 years—half his life!—in Chinese prisons inside Tibet.

Margaret, you look appalled. Yes, I was too when I heard his story. And more so when I learned how much company he had, and still has.

His crime was something that you and I take for granted: Wanting the freedom to worship his own God.

Let me take you back a bit. When Palden was a child, he dreamed of becoming a monk, studying at a monastery, and of some day traveling to Lhasa, the capital city of Tibet, a holy place—and the home of the Dalai Lama. He accomplished all these things.

He got to Lhasa at a time when the Chinese were taking over Tibet. He joined other monks in a nonviolent rally. With them, he was arrested and put in prison. Palden was told he would be released if he would denounce the Dalai Lama and pledge loyalty to the new Chinese government. He refused.

I wonder how many of us would have had the courage to do that?

Several classmates volunteered comments: Margaret said, "This is a little like the situation with the Khmer Rouge." Tom intervened, "Not quite because the Chinese are targeting these monks, not the overall population, right?" Then, Pam said, "They are specific targets, but maybe as a way of reaching the overall populace. See what you think after you hear the rest of the story."

After several years in prison, Palden escaped, fleeing on foot through the snowy mountains. He made it to within one mile of the Bhutan border before he was captured by Chinese police. He was returned to prison and put in solitary confinement.

Needless to say, prison life was a horror. There were long interrogations every day, and food was rationed to starvation proportions. Sometimes prisoners were beaten by guards, and sometimes they were forced to participate in what they called struggle sessions. Does anyone want to venture a guess as to what a struggle session is?

"Something pretty grim," said classmate Jerome.

You're right. A struggle session is when they call all the prisoners into the courtyard. The guards select one prisoner and tell everyone he has committed some crime. The prisoners are forced to ridicule and beat the chosen one until he confesses to a crime he did not commit. The confession adds time to his sentence. If you don't participate in the struggle session, you will be selected next. Worse, your family may be harmed. [There were exclamations and sounds of disbelief from the audience, to which Pam responded with, "Yes," and a deep sigh.]

During his years in prison, Palden witnessed other monks commit suicide, and he spoke of nuns being raped and beaten by the Chinese guards.

Eventually, they did release him. After 33 years in prison, Margaret, Palden was allowed to return home—a home that no longer existed. Then, with the help of friends, he was able to escape from Tibet, fulfill his dream, and meet with the Dalai Lama, who now lives in exile in India. As you can see on this map, the journey through the mountains from Tibet to India is long and rugged. Nevertheless, he got there.

Palden has just published a book about his life, titled *Fire Under the Snow*. I brought it with me to show you. [Class reacts as the book is passed around.] I strongly recommend that everyone read it. The book focuses on how his rights were taken away. It's hard to imagine how we'd feel if our rights were taken away.

[Pause.]

For example, is anyone here Catholic? [Jerome raises his hand.] Okay, Jerome. How would you feel if you were told you could no longer believe in the pope? Or that the pope could no longer live in the Vatican?

Leslie, how would you feel if you were told you could only have one child, that if you became pregnant again you would be forced to abort? [Leslie reacts.] In China, the rule is one child to a family.

To know how much this man endured has put a sadness in my heart that is hard to describe. At our organization, we all feel the same sadness.

END

The purpose of our company is to allow Tibetans like Palden to realize their dreams. To know what freedom is, to be able to send their child to a good school, or to receive medical treatment the same as anyone else. And most importantly, to let people like you and me know that there are Tibetans like Palden Gyatso in prison today.

By concentrating on dialoguing, seeking and getting response throughout her presentation, Pam lessened her fear of speaking. She and her audience became involved in a tragedy far greater than any they had lived through. It was a shared experience. Her shaking subsided, too. She took the leap over the chasm by building direct questions into her speech.

She requested answers, and by doing that, got her listeners actively involved. She de-isolated herself and found warmth and comfort in real person-to-person exchange.

Using dialogue, Pam truly moved her listeners. She made an impact. She broke down the wall of fear.

Assignment Three

Give a five- to eight-minute talk to three or more people, in which you will try to dialogue with your listeners throughout the presentation.

1. Choose a topic you know about, something that matters to you.
2. Plan to structure the middle first, then the end, then the beginning.
3. Decide how you will get a response. After the opening response-getter, plan to seek a response from your listeners every three to four minutes. Encourage reactions from your audience—comments, questions, answers to questions, verbal exclamations. Welcome interruptions. You can guide the dialogue because you are at the helm.
4. Use at least five dialoguing devices described in this step.
5. Practice your presentation out loud. Stand, holding your outline in your hand. (Get used to doing this because some venues may not have a lectern.)
6. Tape-record your practice session. Listen to it. See if you hear clarity, response (your response to the imagined audience's response), involvement. Do this several times, until you feel in control. Then . . .
7. You're on! Go out and give the speech. Record it.
8. Listen to the tape, and answer the questions in the Self-Critique Questionnaire for Step Three.
9. Practice Voice Exercise #3, and Voice Exercises #1 and #2 leading up to it (see Appendix A).

Self-Critique Questionnaire for Step Three

▶ Did I stay with my outline? If I went off of it, when did it happen? Did something good come of that?

▶ When and how did I build a dialogue with my listeners?

▶ How good a sleuth was I? Did I walk around into the audience (literally or figuratively) or did I stay hidden behind the lectern?

▶ What could I do next time to make it better?

▶ What were the parts of the discussion that excited me the most?

SCHEDULE FOR WORKSHOP #3

1. Do Voice Exercises #1, #2, and #3 (in the "Voice Work" appendix) as a group. (Remember to do them daily, as well.)

2. Go around the room and have each person give his or her prepared speech to the entire group.

3. After everyone has finished, take a few minutes and answer your Self-Critique Questionnaire for Step Three, and share your answers with the group. Continue to give and take criticism constructively.

4. Read through Assignment Four together.

5. *Homework:* Read Step Four and prepare to do Assignment Four at the next meeting.

Note: For the next three meetings (Steps Four, Five, and Six) you'll need to try to increase the number of people in your audience. Since the group won't be getting any larger, it would be ideal to *rehearse* your speech in front of the group next week, and then plan to deliver it (if possible) to a group larger than the workshop (e.g., at work, a family get-together, a PTA meeting, a town council meeting, a bridal shower). For the final step—Step Seven— you should each be thinking about guests you can bring to your workshop so that for your final speech, you'll have a more realistic audience, not just the members of your group.

▼

Tap Your Creativity

Behind making your own stuff
there's another level: making your
own tools to make your own stuff.

STEWART BRAND

To create, says the dictionary, is to make or bring into existence something new, to produce something fresh and unique using imaginative skill.

Our ability to create defines us as humans. It is a power each of us possesses. When it is unleashed and finally allowed to soar, it becomes our life force.

Tapping into your creativity is essential to overcoming your fear of speaking. When you are completely engaged in and enthralled by what you are communicating, when your senses are heightened and your imagination is in high gear, there simply is no room for fear.

And when the fear is gone, speaking in public becomes an exciting experience; it becomes *fun!* The vistas open to you are endless.

I like the description of how creativity is used in her corporation day by day, offered by Anthea Disney, CEO of Newscorp:

> Where I work, creativity is a natural part of the thought process. It's integral, not separate from what we do every day.
>
> We do it automatically. We do it by instinct but also by training. We apply it to everything, large and small, from writing clever headlines to colossal ideas that extend the empire.

Fearless speakers, too, allow their creative juices to flow freely—indeed, they depend on those juices.

Creativity isn't just an exercise in manufacturing external gimmicks and devices. It doesn't mean merely enlivening your "show" or adding trappings and ornaments just because they're fancy and pretty. Or pressuring yourself to turn your "performance" into a theatrical tour de force.

Instead, what I am talking about is using your own *innate* creativity to express what you think and feel. With your creativity, you can energize yourself and your listeners, too. You can get so involved in sharing your idea, your insight, your story, your solution, that your fear of speaking vanishes.

And out of that process, amazing things can come.

The Wide World of Creativity

I define creativity in the broadest possible sense. Those among us who are gifted singers, writers, painters, and actors haven't cornered the market on creativity. There is creative potential in any human undertaking, including business, government, social service, the arts, and homemaking. Creativity leads to invention and to solutions of problems.

Businesses that fail to encourage creativity and recognize its value are doomed to stagnate.

Those businesses that see themselves enthusiastically participating in the never-ending creative renewal of society will flourish in the new millennium. Talent will be drawn magnetically to companies like this.

And the spirit of this talent—and of the leadership that nurtures it—will be nowhere more evident than in the public presentations made by the fearless speakers among them.

I am amazed every day at the evidence of entrepreneurial creativity that surrounds me. A few examples:

- Hermès of Paris, makers of pricey leather goods, has devised a nifty leather carrying case for one of the most famous inventions of the late twentieth century—the Post-it®. Now the stylish businessperson on the go need not be without that favorite sticky source of written reminders.

- The Disney Company, with a little help from the city of New York, has restored the New Amsterdam Theatre on 42nd

Street and turned it into a commercially successful entertainment venue. This is just one such theater restoration project. There are many others, in cities such as Cleveland, St. Louis, Detroit, Chicago, Miami, Los Angeles, and Toronto. Who would have guessed, 30 years ago, that these seemingly doomed entertainment palaces could be saved, much less turned into real businesses?

- The book you are reading, I am pleased to report, is no farther away from its market than a few strokes on a computer keyboard—you can order it online. Thousands of books—virtually everything in print—are available this way. So are countless compact disc recordings and videos—original Broadway cast albums and movies.
- And speaking of compact discs: Everywhere I go I see people walking plugged into Walkmen, listening to their favorite music through headphones. It reminds me of the billion-dollar electronic invention of yesteryear—the transistor radio. Imagine! When I was in first grade the principal of the Delano Grammar School in Chicago, Mr. Wilson, predicted, "One day, we'll be able to listen to a radio so small it will fit right into your shirt pocket!"
- It wasn't that long ago that suitcases had no wheels.
- And why did it take so long for someone to invent that accordion cardboard device that fits inside the windshield and shades the seats and steering wheel of a car during scorching heat?

If we were having this discussion in class, I know that by now you would be volunteering examples of your own—creative ideas and enterprises that amaze and inspire you.

It's fun to vicariously relish other people's creative successes, and to think about how they've affected our culture and daily business lives.

What I would ask you to do now, if we were face to face, is to try to transfer that enthusiasm to your own life. You, too, are creative, regardless of whether you know it. You can apply your own creativity to your work, your community service, your social life.

Even within the most staid businesses, there is plenty of room for creative energy to come into play. And wise executives know when to encourage it. The following story is an example.

KATHERINE'S STORY
You Oughta Be in Pictures

Katherine, a student in my class at the New School, works in the accounting office of a large banking firm known for its financial acumen, not necessarily its sense of humor.

When asked why she was taking the class, Katherine said, "Presentations are not my strong suit. I try to *avoid* them. When I can't, I put off preparing for them until the last minute and then I'm very uncomfortable because I haven't prepared properly."

The fourth assignment in class was to do a speech in a business setting in which you *tap your creativity*. Katherine's hobby was collecting vintage films and still photographs from them. She decided to prepare a presentation for the Annual Marketing Strategy meeting. She gathered the stills and put them on a videotape, with captions that good-naturedly joshed her colleagues: a photo of Harrison Ford in the path of a giant rolling boulder in *Raiders of the Lost Ark*, captioned "Jack Johnson takes over as VP-Marketing, and hits the ground running"; the crew of the starship *Enterprise* from *Star Trek*, captioned "This year's New Market Development Committee." The laughter she created made the presentation energetic and memorable.

She had fun with the assignment and couldn't wait to get to work on it. This was a new experience for someone so accustomed to avoiding making a presentation.

Katherine accomplished two things. First, she reminded her buddies of their responsibilities at the firm, and at the same time showed her understanding of the pressures they were under at the meeting. Second, she found a way of using her hobby, collecting vintage films, to overcome the fear brought on by avoidance.

Your Creative Resources

Think about your hobbies and how you can use them for professional purposes. Collecting coins, Indian artifacts, old prints of your hometown. Perhaps you can find a way to work your passion for ballroom dancing into your next speech. Because it is part of your lifestyle, it won't seem like work. You will prepare well in advance and avoid the fear of avoidance.

People who work within the walls of supposedly uncreative organizations—financial institutions, government agencies, law firms,
electronics manufacturers, and insurance companies, for example—
have wells of creativity within them. These wells often go untapped,
and that is a loss, both to their employers and to themselves. When
they are explored and used, it becomes evident that fear of speaking
and creativity simply cannot exist within the same person at the
same time. Creativity takes over and pushes fear of speaking away
because when you're busy creating parallels of one of your colleagues
with movie stars, you're involved in an activity that makes you and
your audience laugh.

Start with Your Senses

You experience the world through your five senses: sight, sound,
taste, touch, and smell. Language helps us to communicate what we
experience. Thus sensory experience and language are linked.

Perhaps the most famous illustration of the creativity in this link
between language and our senses is found in the early life of Helen
Keller, the first deaf and blind person to learn language and master
literacy.

In the play and later in the movie version of the story of her life,
The Miracle Worker, the climactic scene is the moment when she
discovers that her teacher, Annie Sullivan, is touching her hand for
a purpose.

All the years before that moment, Helen's world had been chaos.
She had no way of identifying or communicating with the object she
touched, the sensations she felt, the people she experienced. But
one day Sullivan got the idea to spell W-A-T-E-R into her hand,
while allowing water to flow over her wrist. Helen made the connection. Her sensations, her reality, suddenly had meaning. Taste,
touch, and smell became channels of learning for her.

Thanks to Sullivan's innovative teaching, Helen Keller found her
voice. She will forever influence our perception of what one can do
with the use of only three of the five senses.

We who see, hear, speak, and write take for granted the myriad
sensations of the day and the language we use to communicate
them.

You can use your five senses to build creative ways to tell your story, to get your feelings and thoughts—what you care most about—across to your listeners.

1. The visuals you create to illustrate your talk, such as pictures, graphs, slides, artifacts, will appeal to your listener's sense of *sight*. For instance, PowerPoint software is used to sell real estate. You can create images of homes showing various land-scaping effects, enlarge the square footage, indicate where the swimming pool might be, and more. It's fun and practical. You don't have to travel miles to see the property.

2. On a CBS *Sunday Morning* story, Barbara Kingsolver, a novelist, describes the setting in which she writes. I found her use of language to describe what she *hears* particularly vivid and moving. "Appalachia is a place where I write. Between May and August our family settles here. We pace the porch while rain pummels the tin roof. And when it stops, we listen to a concert of dripping leaves and the indignant Carolina wrens reclaiming their damp territories. Then come the wood thrushers, heartbreakers, with their minor-keyed harmonies." Kingsolver incorporates this sensuality into her communication.

3. At an IPO offering, the CEO of Coleman, Inc., demonstrated the value of a Coleman cooler to put in the trunk of your car. He carefully lifted the heavy cooler, opened it, and took out the various articles in it—flashlight, portable generator, camping tools, and more. *Touching* and showing how to use the products were very effective selling tools. It connected the audience to the presentation and encouraged response.

4. As part of a TV interview, Leonard Lauder, chairman and chief executive officer of Estée Lauder Companies, described how he and his wife, Evelyn Lauder, senior corporate vice president of Estée Lauder Companies, choose the scents that they use in their fragrances. "We use the finest essential oils that come from many different sources—distilled from woods such as sandalwood or patchouli; fruits, citrus notes such as grapefruit, lemon, mandarin. Notes are individual elements within a fragrance which are blended together to create a unique new

composition, much like notes in music are combined to create new musical creations."

Mrs. Lauder uses special equipment that's designed to analyze and capture the aura of certain essences as they exist in nature. For example, she uses it to capture the essence of a certain type of orchid that she grows in her garden. These essences are then blended into fragrances for perfumes, shower gels, body lotions, candles, solid perfumes, and many other products. Both Evelyn and Leonard Lauder have highly refined senses of *smell* along with a unique ability to envision creative fragrance effects.

5. Carol Prager, a cookbook author and food writer, describes the many sublime dishes she had in Italy. Her favorite was a pasta indigenous to Umbria with a sauce called *arrabiatta*. Made from ripe, fresh tomatoes, a pinch of red pepper flakes, extra virgin olive oil, and salt, the long fresh strands of pasta, like thick spaghetti, had just the right texture, not al dente. You cook dry pasta al dente (firm to the bite), but fresh pasta should be tender. "My favorite foods don't need much adornment, just ingredients that are at the peak of their flavor." Carol said, "Each ingredient was so fresh—the freshly pressed olive oil, and as soon as I *tasted* the sauce, I knew immediately that they were fresh plum tomatoes. Even the type of salt they use is different. Just as the waitress swung around the table and I saw the dish, my mouth started to water."

Your senses help you overcome fear because when you get involved with your senses—sight, sound, touch, taste, and smell—you experience and share something that is real, and you're no longer afraid.

This step asks you to embrace your senses as a way of opening a new door to creativity. If you speak from your whole experience, sensory as well as intellectual, you will feel whole, be whole, and get the response you want from your listeners fearlessly. You will be eager to share your creativity. It will be fun to do, and it will lessen, if not entirely eliminate, panic, because you're involved in something you truly like to do.

The Fearless Speaker's Creative Tools

If speaking in public has always been your idea of a nightmare, you probably regard tools such as rich language, evocative props, and physical movement as niceties that are beyond your reach. After all, it's hard to think about onomatopoeia, fossils, Indian arrowheads, or hand gestures that describe your product if you're sweating and shaking. But I am here to tell you that the use of your five senses is what will help you overcome your fear. Your innate creativity is like natural Dramamine!

Listen to your voice, the way you express yourself in private, the relish with which you choose an anecdote or a detail in telling a story. You know to whom you are speaking and what, exactly, you want to communicate.

Word Pictures

Rita, a student, talked about ice skating in class. Her goal was to encourage everyone in the room to go to Rockefeller Center, rent some skates, and get on the rink. She loved the sport and loved talking about it.

But, she said, she always panicked when she had to speak, and couldn't tolerate standing still in front of a class. She said she is most at ease when moving, which is why she loves ice skating in the first place. The trouble was that, as a conservative corporate executive, she often had to give presentations either seated at a conference table or from behind a lectern, and this physical restraint made her vocally restrained.

To compromise, we experimented with letting her words do the gliding and swooping and soaring; we incorporated a sense of movement into her language. Here's how she described her experience ice skating on a frozen canal in Holland: Her upper body swayed and her arms followed through. She was freed and our senses were aroused.

> The air was damp but comforting, like a blanket. I heard it whisking by me. I felt my skates cutting the air and the ice, but quietly, serenely. I kept moving through the air. And I remembered Carl Sandburg's poem: "The fog comes on little cat feet . . ."

In her imagination, Rita was back on the ice in Holland. Through her words, we were with her. And as she told her story of moving across the ice, she was gliding in her imagination, too—leaving her panic behind.

Maura, another victim of panic, also found relief in evocative word pictures. Here's her highly personalized description of her hometown, Pittsburgh, Pennsylvania:

> I am going to talk about my favorite neighborhood in Pittsburgh, which is a small Italian neighborhood. There were so many churches in the area and all the churches had a lot of different statues of the saints and they just loomed very quietly in the morning. You could hear the sound that the wind would make when it blew across the suspension cables of the West End Bridge. There's a little Italian bakery there. . . . In the morning the bakers come out and take cigarette breaks. . . . They would just be wearing bakers' whites and tees. . . . You could look down from Island Avenue, it's a very steep bluff, on what used to be the steam repair shop. . . . It's still there and has 24 Roman basilica windows. Early in the morning there's a yellow cracked light that's very eerie and comforting at the same time. . . . In the summer we used to sit on our porch at night and the night hawks and bats would come up from the creek and the ravine. You could look down on that ravine and it was just a big vast bowl of light from all the lightning bugs . . .

Vivid Language and Business

Well, fine you say, as long as the subject of your presentation lends itself to such dramatic and literary treatment. Most business presentations don't.

Is that so? Well, look at this excerpt from IBM chairman Lou Gerstner's 1998 address to his shareholders:

> The resurgence in our storage business continued in 1997 due in large measure to our technology leadership in disk drives. Our teams established new world records for storage densities and delivered the world's highest-capacity PC drives. They're about the size of an audiocassette, but they hold the equivalent of a stack of printed paper higher than the John Hancock Building. That's pretty good. But I've told our storage teams that this year I want that stack to be higher than the Sears Tower.

Gerstner, one of the best public speakers in America's fraternity of CEOs, used a metaphor to illustrate the capacity of the IBM disk drives. Metaphors, similes, and easy-to-understand analogies are both fun and informative. And they communicate the enthusiasm of the speaker for his or her subject.

Look back on any business presentation you've done in the last year, and you'll probably find opportunities you missed to enliven and personalize passages.

Al, a Wall Street analyst with a penchant for perfectionism, said he dreaded giving oral quarterly reports—explaining current economic trends with handouts full of graphs and statistics. Jazzing up this numbing material seemed impossible.

I asked him to explain a quarterly report to us as though we were in his son's high school class, using a metaphor to describe the current market. He came in with a speech comparing the market to his daily commute: "How many of you have ever commuted to work by train or subway?" he began, getting a response. Then:

> Sometimes when we are waiting for the train we look down the tracks and see the light approaching. And just every once in a while, instead of slowing, the train will barrel past the station without even stopping.
>
> In many ways, today's economy is like that train we see coming toward us. We know that it is currently moving at a high speed. We hope that it will slow down, but some fear that it will continue to accelerate, get off the track and come crashing down in a recession.

Al's delight in the fresh approach to dry material was infectious. Afterward he said the subway metaphor opened up his thinking and allowed him to explain his work "in a way that seemed human, and much more involving." He forgot about being "perfect."

Literary, historical, and pop culture references—if handy and apt—are always good. But don't knock yourself out digging them up. If they come to mind by themselves, arising from your own reading and interests, they'll sound like you. In describing your law firm you might say:

> We're the kind of law firm John Grisham would love to write about. Last year, we defended over 100 indigent clients in federal and local courts, and obtained acquittals or favorable judgments in more than 80 percent of the cases.

As in good writing, the active voice is preferable to the passive voice, and action verbs more effective and efficient than lots of adjectives. For example:

Passive: "New ways to make life easier in the kitchen for the American homemaker have been devised by our product development department."

Active: "Our product development department has devised several new ways to make life in the kitchen easier for the American homemaker."

And:

Dull and unconvincing: "Our great company, bigger and better than ever, is selling more of its excellent product than our competition again this year."

Lively and convincing: "The public devoured our new product line this year, and once more we rolled over the competition."

But don't worry about composing a narrative that sounds like it came out of a novel. Sound like you are talking to your friends and neighbors intelligently with enthusiasm and conviction.

Make Visuals Your Own

Your choice of visuals—slides, photographs, objects, handouts—like your choice of language, should reflect your unique sense of the world. Let visuals ground you and give you a sense of belonging, of warmth and familiarity. Your visual environment can deisolate you.

Look at your office. You've personalized your work space to make it your own. You probably have photographs of your family on your desk. On the shelves may be an assortment of plants, a sports trophy, a piece of pottery you bought in Cancún. On the wall are a framed photograph of your sailboat and, stuck on with tape, a recent political cartoon you believe is right on the money.

Personalize the visuals of your speech, too. Slides you have handchosen, postcards, the poster you brought back all the way from

Moscow, the antique toys your father played with—all will have special meaning when you introduce and describe them.

Some examples, from my students, follow.

MARY JO, LISA, TODD, AND JUDITH'S STORY
A Report Card, Medals, Gold Leaf, and TV Film

Mary Jo, another Wall Street analyst, also struggled with that most routine of presentational chores, the quarterly report. Trying hard to swallow her career terror, she dutifully passed around the company's folder of handouts—graphs, pie charts, and lists—illustrating the financial status she meant to explain.

But she felt trapped rather than liberated by her company's handouts. And when she talked about them, rather than look up and talk to her listeners, she buried her head in her outline. Seeing that, I asked her to come up with a new visual.

And she did. She supplemented the company package of material with a little brochure she designed and wrote herself—a folded chart she called the "Report Card." She explained:

> Like many of you, when I was in elementary school, I anticipated report card day with fear and hope. I will never forget the first time I came home with straight A's.
>
> The report card you have in front of you is a guide to this quarter's financial statement. You can fill it out as we go along. But I am thrilled to tell you in advance, this is going to be another one of those straight A's. We had a wonderful quarter.

When Mary Jo incorporated her own visual, the Report Card, into the presentation, she added something of herself that opened up the moment. She sounded like a different person. She talked to us, not to the lectern. Later, she said it was easier than any other presentation she had ever done.

Lisa, like ice skater executive Rita, would rather be on the move than standing still in front of a group talking with a trembling voice. Lisa is a runner whose greatest joy is the 26-mile footrace known as the marathon. She's very good at it—and has the medals to prove it.

Lisa got rid of her tremulous voice by practicing the voice exercises. When she spoke of running, she brought along her medals and let people hold them and examine them while she told the stories of what it took to win them—imagining herself at the head of the pack in a marathon.

Todd, a Wall Street broker, loved doing business over the phone or in small meetings. But when he had to address a group of six or more people, his hands shook noticeably. He avoided these larger groups whenever possible. But he knew he had to face the fear, or it would impede his career. Tapping his creativity by turning to a series of props helped Todd get over these fears.

Since his private passion is furniture restoration, and he is a seasoned expert, Todd brought in strips of gold leaf, which he would use to gild a picture frame, and showed them as he explained his company's philosophy on long-term investments:

> This gold leaf is very fragile, almost dust. But its value increases with each painstaking layer that gilds the frame. Neither the gold leaf nor the frame is very valuable alone. But if I combine them artfully, I create something unique, of great value.
>
> The same can be said for the way we design long-term investment. We design it with careful craftsmanship, and double the value with our design."

Todd made his point eloquently, and his hands—holding something he truly valued that illustrated his point—remained steady for the first time.

Judith, a student who worked at the United Nations, came to class with a speech detailing human rights abuses. She was very committed to her work on behalf of human rights—and to the speech. But she lost her sense of direction—and became even more fearful—the minute she launched into facts and figures about the various political regimes involved.

She said she feels "lost in all the material, and ineffectual, and then my stomach just knots up."

She needed something concrete, a task that would illustrate her point and anchor her in the moment. She came back to class and showed selected segments from a TV film of the civil strife in Bosnia. *Shot Through the Heart* was a realistic description of the horror of war that best friends suffered. It made these best friends enemies. It almost destroyed their lives (and in one instance did). The story was so dramatic and involving that when Judith presented it her fear of speaking vanished.

Being creative brings you to another level of expression. It elevates your horizons, gives you a sense of self-worth, and involves your listeners.

MICHAEL'S COMPELLING EXAMPLE OF FEARLESS SPEAKING
Peace and the River

Michael, a law student, told us on the first day of class that speaking in public was his greatest fear. He hated being a captive of the *panic* that consumed him, yet couldn't imagine experiencing speaking any other way. He told me later that he seriously considered taking medication that day to calm himself, but decided against it.

Consequently, he amazed himself when he gave this illustrated presentation—not only without fear, but with a feeling of joy he'd never thought possible.

The assignment was to share your greatest passion with the class. Michael chose to talk about his greatest passion: fly-fishing. A trout stream, he said, was the one place he could feel completely at peace. In his speech, he used his creativity to bring us with him, into a serene world where everything was in harmony with nature:

> How many of you have seen *A River Runs Through It* with Robert Redford? [Some people raise their hands.] A touching and well-made film. I think thousands fell in love with fly-fishing by watching that movie.
>
> Today I'm going to try to do three things:
>
> 1. Explain what fly fishing is;
>
> 2. Explain why fly fishing is so appealing to me; and
>
> 3. Give you some information on how you can get started.

MIDDLE

The difference between traditional fishing casting lures or bait, which have weight, and fly-fishing casting tiny life-size replicas of real flies, which have no weight.

> Traditional fishing doesn't work well on trout. Trout are too smart to take big metal hooks and lures, like these. . . . I'd like to pass around this box containing large fish hooks and shiny lures.

Trout are very picky about their diet. What they like is aquatic insects like these. . . .

Michael passed around a box with a see-through plastic cover containing tiny flies, all carefully mounted on pins.

These are mayflies, caddisflies, stoneflies. Each about an eighth of an inch long, and light as air.

How do they stay on the hook? The answer is, they don't. So what do we do about that? We don't use them. Instead, we make our own flies with hooks built in. Exact imitations, like these. . . .

He passed around another box, this one containing handmade flies, replicas of the real thing. Then he took one out of the box, held it gingerly between two fingers for a moment, admiring it, before placing it in the palm of his hand. One of his personal creations.

Remember, trout are smart. You can't fool them with wood and plastic. We make our flies out of natural materials—animal hair, feathers, fur. And they have to be just right. More on that in a minute.

Next, we have a physics problem to solve. How do you throw something that weighs almost nothing? Here, try it, Alice.

Alice took the fly Michael offered and tried to throw it. Of course, it went nowhere, just fluttered to the floor.

This is where the physics problem kicks in. Since you can't sneak up on a trout without scaring it, you have to cast the lure to the fish from far away, like 20 to 100 feet. How can you do that when the fly weighs almost nothing? Here's how: The line, not the lure, is weighted. Here is a sample of a weighted fly line.

Michael gave us a wonderfully vivid description of how a fly line is cast—the overhead back-and-forth whipping motion as the line gathers momentum, the graceful flight of the line with the fly at its end, unfurling over the sun-flecked water.

The fly on the end is just along for the ride. The line would travel the same distance whether the insect is on the end or not.

It's a thrilling thing to do—to make that line go out, and uncoil, and place the fly so gently on the surface of the water. It's beautiful. And that brings me to my final point.

END

Why do people do this? Why do I do it?

> First, I do it for the mental challenge. You have to pick the right fly to use. That means it must be the exact kind of insect the trout is feeding on. And that varies, not only by season and location, but by what stream you are in, what day it is, what time of day it is!

Michael broke out his books and charts here and showed us cross sections of streams at different times of the day, and photos and drawings of insects in various stages of development.

> I like the physical challenge, too. Casting skillfully—that takes practice. [He demonstrated, with a fly rod and an imaginary line.] And, believe it or not, there is such a thing as wading well. Wade poorly— go to the wrong place and make a lot of noise—and it's good-bye fish.
>
> You must become a part of the natural environment. And that is the best reason to fly-fish. Wading around in a stream, quietly, for hours, produces many spiritually satisfying moments. It gives you a perspective that is rare—a view as a participant in nature, rather than just as observer.

Long before his big finish, Michael had already sold us. We could see ourselves hip-deep in rushing clean water, dappled light on our faces, a fly line snaking silently from our rod.

But, more important, Michael sold himself—on the certain knowledge that he can speak fearlessly. After his talk, we all had questions and comments. Flushed with his success, he answered them all with warmth and authority. Robert Redford himself couldn't have done better.

What made Michael's presentation so compelling was the blend of his authority and passion, and the cherished flies, equipment, books, and other things—all among his prized possessions—that he brought to give new dimension to his words.

When Michael tapped his creativity and filled his presentation with it, there was no room left for fear—and no need for medication.

You may be thinking, "Okay, fine. A guy gives a talk about trout fishing and he gets rid of his fear of speaking because he is very creative. How does that help me when I am strapped into a five-minute presentation on Global Syndicated Finance full of jargon, numbers, and comparisons with nary a fly (real or fake) around and nothing that is creative?"

Answer:

1. Find a way to connect to what you're saying. That connection will evidence itself in your enthusiasm and belief in what you are saying.
2. If you can simplify the jargon or make it clearer, all the better. Hopefully, your slides will help clarify, not duplicate, your text.
3. When you say the numbers and comparisons, relish them, build to a climactic number, unravel the comparisons as if they were clues in an exciting mystery novel.
4. Find a metaphor, analogy, or other creative way to put your unique touch on the material.

In other words, internalize the presentation so that it truly means something to you. You then become eager to share it. The focus is off of you and onto the content.

Assignment Four

Give a talk of at least eight minutes to five to eight people, using visual aids and other creative resources.

1. Choose a topic with which you can be creative visually and/or with language.
2. Plan your talk starting with the middle, then the end, then the beginning.
3. Use one of your creative tools to get your initial response. To establish and maintain dialogue throughout, use each of the creative tools described in this step starting on page 84 and any others you may think of.
4. Use the creative devices to support, dramatize, and illustrate each point in the middle section or body of your presentation.
5. *Important:* Try to include something that arouses each of the five senses at least once. In addition, use metaphors, similes, and descriptive language.

6. Practice with a tape recorder. Listen to the tape and critique yourself.

7. You're on! Go out and give the speech. Record it.

8. Listen to the tape, and fill out the Self-Critique Questionnaire for Step Four.

9. Practice Voice Exercise #4 and the three voice exercises leading up to it (see Appendix A).

Self-Critique Questionnaire for Step Four

▶ What new ways did I discover to make my points?

▶ Which creative techniques did I use? How was each received?

▶ What new language did I find—images individual to me—to express my ideas?

▶ How did the creativity exhilarate me?

▶ What creative technique worked best?

SCHEDULE FOR WORKSHOP #4

1. Do Voice Exercises #1, #2, #3, and #4 as a group.

2. Go around the room and have each person give his or her prepared speech to the entire group.

3. After everyone has finished, take a few minutes and answer your Self-Critique Questionnaire for Step Four, and share your answers with the group. Continue to give and take criticism constructively.

4. Read through Assignment Five together.

5. *Homework:* Read Step Five and prepare to do Assignment Five at the next meeting.

▼

Learn to Persuade

By persuading others, we
convince ourselves.

JUNIUS

The final three steps in the Seven Step Program—Learn to Persuade, Achieve Your Higher Objective, and Give the Gift of Your Conviction—are closely linked. After you have studied and practiced all three, you will automatically integrate them and perform them as if they were one.

Here's what you have to look forward to.

The Fearless Speaker's Heart Connection

- Step Five, Learn to Persuade, helps you tell your listeners: "Here is *what* I want you to do . . ."
- Step Six, Achieve Your Higher Objective, explains: "This is *why* I want you to do it . . ."
- Step Seven, Give the Gift of Your Conviction, reveals: "I feel this way *because* . . ."

These three steps work together like this.

Tom, who has a son in the fifth grade, gives a talk to the PTA fathers, urging them to sponsor a Saturday morning car wash, in which dads and kids would work together.

He tells them how much fun it will be, how much money the students can make for a field trip to a museum, and how little preparation time is involved. But here is his clincher: "Of all the positive reasons I've given you to do this . . . there is one reason I haven't mentioned that outweighs the rest: I want to have this experience with my son. It will be good for us to do this together—and, I think, good for you and your sons and daughters, too."

Why did Tom try to **persuade** the group to organize the car wash? He wants them to take that action because he knows it will deepen their relationships to their children. His **objective** is to build a bond with his own son and encourage other parents to build a similar bond by spending time with their children. And why is Tom's **conviction** on this matter so strong? Because, he confides to his wife and close friends, he never had experiences like this with his own father, and he feels the pain of lost opportunities.

To understand how these three steps work together, however, it's necessary at this point in your journey to fearless speaking to break them down and consider them separately.

The first is Step Five, Learn to Persuade. The mental and emotional muscles you will develop as you learn and practice the skills of persuasion will strengthen you as a fearless speaker, no matter what your topic or objective.

Persuasive speaking invariably becomes fearless speaking. When you are completely involved in what you are saying and you have a good road map, the fear is crowded out. When your mind is totally engaged in your mission, there simply is no room for the old terror.

In this step, think about persuasion, not just as an exercise in manipulative salesmanship or formal debate, but as a way of connecting to your core, to what matters to you today. And then express that connection to others. Invite your audience to relate to how you think and feel, to understand the truth in what you have to say.

This is crucial in helping you overcome your fear of speaking. When your focus is on changing someone's thinking, the fear is replaced by your energy and enthusiasm for your cause.

SANJAY'S STORY
Finding His Roots

Sanjay did not get admitted to medical school the first time he applied. That rejection shattered his confidence. He took a year off in New York City trying different jobs and courses. He couldn't face a second rejection. He wasn't clear about why he wanted to go to medical school. He wasn't sure of himself. He just knew in his heart that he loved medicine.

That is why he took the course I teach to help people overcome the fear of speaking. He said it helped him regain the confidence to apply to another medical school.

After the course ended, Sanjay e-mailed me that he had been accepted. I was thrilled for him. The feeling of being accepted has helped him overcome his career terror, and his fear of speaking has begun to diminish.

When Sanjay first came to class, he barely spoke above a whisper; his speeches were not organized and had little dimension to them. But his subject matter was always potent.

Now that he is in medical school, he still feels uneasy about speaking, but he has learned how to put his thoughts together and his voice is more purposeful. In the following speech, Sanjay demonstrates beautifully how sincere persuasion can turn fearful speaking into fearless speaking.

Born and reared in America by immigrant Indian parents, Sanjay traveled to India during the summer to visit his extended family. There he spent time with relatives he had never met, in a culture that was both foreign and familiar to him.

BEGINNING

Response-getter: "Did you travel this summer, Leslie? Paul? Where did you go?" (They respond.) Sanjay told us he traveled to India to visit his extended family. And, despite the high cost of the trip, he was very happy that he did.

Sanjay's persuasion aim: To urge us to reach out to our families and spend time with them.

Sanjay's persuasion strategy: To testify to his need to reconnect with his own family.

MIDDLE

- In India, Sanjay found his cultural roots.
- But what was even better was discovering how much, on a fundamental human level, he needed to get support from his family.

- He described movingly the moments that bonded him to his family:

    Playing soccer with his cousins

    Staying up all night with them and listening to music they all loved on the radio

    Dancing with his aunt amid the clean sheets she had just hung on a clothesline

- Putting off fulfilling that need would have left a void in him. He would not have been able to do his work in school as well and live a full, rich life.

 END

- Don't postpone connecting with your family.

- Especially if your extended family is in another land, and of another culture. We can't know what the world beyond our shores is like today unless we go and see for ourselves.

- Sanjay came home feeling connected to his family and to a much larger family—the Family of Man.

Without gimmicks or melodramatic flourishes, Sanjay kept us with him through these familial moments. We rewarded Sanjay, not just with applause, but with a flurry of questions and personal responses to his talk. And when we reviewed it all on video, Sanjay made a remarkable discovery: Somewhere along the way, his fear had vanished. He was elated, and so were we.

Sanjay's presentation worked so well because it was about an experience that moved him deeply—indeed, placed his life and his identity in a new perspective for him—and because he sincerely wanted us to understand.

At the same time, his talk was properly organized. First, he got a response from us, then he took us through his journey step by carefully planned step and prepared us for his conclusion.

At the outset, Sanjay stepped out of his self-imposed isolation. He placed his focus on his purpose and on us, not on himself.

Sanjay had taken an important step toward becoming a fearless speaker.

Who's Listening?

You know how it feels to fear speaking in public . . . to take that long walk to the podium trying to remember what you're going to say . . . to look across the microphone and lectern light for the first time at the faces of the audience.

Who is this audience to you? An "it," or a "they"?

If you are consumed with your fear and struggling just to get through your ordeal, the audience is an "it"—and perhaps, in your mind, a hostile "it," sitting in judgment of you, disapproving of inadequacies you imagine you are revealing.

You know by now that relating to your audience as fellow human beings—speaking to just one, person to person, and by extension speaking to all—is essential for effective and eventually fearless speaking.

It helps immensely, then, to know who these fellow human beings are. And finding out isn't that difficult. It just takes a little advance thinking, and maybe some questions. Depending on your topic and where you are speaking, are you talking to:

- Fellow professionals? Business colleagues? Prospective customers?
- Fellow parents of teenagers? Parents of adopted children? Parents Without Partners?
- Neighbors who share your concern about a needed traffic light? Who disagree among themselves about a proposed increase in school taxes?
- People of your religious faith? Different faiths?
- People who know your city as well as you do? Who are new in town?

Are you asking for money, for instance, for breast cancer research? If so, are you talking to:

- Victims?
- Their families?
- Women at risk?
- People whose lives have never been touched by cancer?
- All of the above?

You may speak differently to each group.

Knowing what matters to the other person—notice I said "person," not "audience"—is essential if you are to speak persuasively and fearlessly.

Ask yourself these key questions:

- *Who* am I talking to?
- *What* do I want to say to them?
- *Why* do I think these people need to hear this from me now?
- *What* do I want them to do?

Be specific when answering the last key question on this list. *Exactly*, what do you want your listeners to do? Do you want them:

- To take a certain action?
- To change an attitude?
- To reflect on a problem in a different way?

On the job, do you want your coworkers for:

- Your new project?
- Reorganizing the department?
- Reclaiming a lost market share?

Knowing exactly what you want from your listeners—what action you want them to take, what new understanding or change of heart you want them to experience—is essential to effective persuasion. This kind of clarity and passion subdues fear.

Your mind will be riveted on action and audience, not anxiety and insecurity.

Your presentation is only as strong as the evidence you present. Think of your talk as an exercise in both show and tell. Imagine you are putting together the main body of a documentary film, in which the narrator *tells* us, in logical order, what is happening, while the camera *shows* evidence to our eyes.

Evidence itself comes from four primary sources:

- Your own experience
- The experience of others as reported to you
- The results of your own research
- The logic of your own reasoning

Here are outlines of short but effective persuasive presentations given by my students. The outlines are arranged just as the students gave them: the beginning first, middle next, then the ending. Let's look through them for:

- Specific arguments (arranged chronologically or topically)
- Major points
- Supporting points
- Reasons, evidence

ANNA'S STORY
Publishing a Magazine

Anna is the editor of a business magazine recently acquired by a large corporation that isn't in the publishing business. As a cost-cutting measure, the new owners demanded a drastically reduced editorial production schedule. That meant Anna would have to put out her magazine in half the usual time—two weeks instead of a month.

Anna had struggled all her adult life to be more assertive. This edict by the new owners sent shivers up her spine. She knew she had to confront her new bosses about the certain consequences of this new schedule.

Avoiding a confrontation would affect the quality of her work and, therefore, the quality of her magazine. She had to weigh her fear of speaking against her need to speak out.

So she faced her fear and arranged a presentation for the new owners, who knew nothing about the editorial process, to persuade them that she really did need a month to publish a quality magazine. She prepared thoroughly and focused on her deep sense of professionalism, with the knowledge that she was right and had something important to say.

Here's how she made her case.

BEGINNING

Response-getter:

> Mr. Brown, did you enjoy the cover story in the last issue? Did you know the story was quoted on *CNN Financial News* yesterday?
>
> Thank you . . . we worked hard on the story. Today I'd like to describe to you how that story came to be, what made it as good as it was.

Anna's persuasion aim:

I'd like to show you what it takes for us to have the kind of impact this magazine is known for.

MIDDLE

Anna's persuasion strategy: To tell, in detail and in chronological order, the story of one magazine article from start to finish. To lead the new owners to the conclusion that four weeks are necessary to publish a quality magazine of 12 articles.

I. Major points:
   A. How a major magazine gets published.
   B. Prove chronologically to the new owners that four weeks are needed to publish a quality magazine.
      1. Pitch by writer or editor, follow-up meetings, assignment given.
      2. How an editor conceptualizes a story: ideas for "lead" (beginning of story) and illustrations; establish and maintain the focus originally decided upon with the writer.
      3. Reporting process
         a. Example of questions that arise
         b. Resolution and problem solving
      4. Editing process
         a. Timely
         b. Accurate
      5. Repeat the all-important concept of proper focus.
II. Reasons and evidence
   A. Multiply the work time for this story by 12, for a full issue.
      1. Photographs
      2. Illustrations
   B. Closing cycle
      1. Send to press
      2. Built-in quality control
   C. Why a month is needed.

END

I. Every step is needed.

II. It takes four weeks to adequately complete one edition of the magazine.

The new owners withdrew their demand.

YAHRON'S COMPELLING EXAMPLE OF FEARLESS SPEAKING
Selling His Satellite Service . . . and Himself

Yahron, an Israeli technology whiz kid, began working for his father's company right out of university. The company specializes in introducing new technologies to emerging foreign markets. Yahron knew he needed help after attending his first board meeting, where he went blank when he tried to speak.

"I know I'm just starting out, but still I feel a lot of pressure to at least seem intelligent," he said. "Instead I felt like I couldn't think. I'm beginning to meet with potential clients, and I've got to get organized. And I worry about my English, my grammar." Career terror reared its ugly head.

Although he attended college in the United States, Yahron knows that when he gets nervous, his language logic goes back and forth between English and his native Hebrew.

His misguided antidote for the panic that overtook him when he needed to speak "perfectly" was to write what he had to say word for word. So he came to his first session armed with a fully written-out text for a presentation he planned to make to potential partners in a combined venture with his father's firm. The presentation introduced a revolutionary new product.

"I'll be meeting with company representatives and introducing myself and the product, and if I can get their interest, then later the heads of the company would meet to discuss the deal," he explained nervously.

"Treat me as the company representative," I said. "Let's go through a mock meeting, with you presenting yourself and the product just as you plan to do with a real client."

He introduced himself very formally, pulled out a three-page, single-spaced text, and began to alternately read and speak it to me. He sounded like a schoolboy reading an essay. His speech was full of detailed, jargon-esque language—for example:

> The revenue benefit of this product is in line with your present oper-
> ating system of prepayment transactions. Due to the anticipated
> demand for the product we consider export risks, such as bureaucratic
> interference, governmental procedures, et cetera, to be negligible. In
> addition we expect our initial sales to be confined to world relief orga-
> nizations with a strong track record for successful delivery to site . . .

He continued with hard-sell assertions such as:

> This product fulfills all your company's requirements, and will allow
> you to realize all revenues prior to expenditure.

As he went on, his voice grew harsh and adamant. His sound
graduated from schoolboy to adolescent bully. The effect was not
convincing.

When he finished I asked, "What is it you want me to do?"

"To get interested in the product! To believe me!" he said, as
though it was obvious.

"Is that why you wrote all this material, and read it to me?"

"Well, I want to make sure the client knows that I know what I'm
talking about, and I need to have the exact words planned because
otherwise I go blank. Also I need to go through all of it without
being interrupted. Then the client can ask questions. If I get interrupted it will throw me off track."

"Turn the pages over so that you can't see them, and tell me about
the product," I told him.

He began to explain, in simple words:

> It's a new system for water testing—for testing the chemicals in water
> sources. Instead of having government or private company inspectors
> go out into remote areas to test irrigation water, and well water, we
> have a kit that is so simple the farmers or village people can use it them-
> selves to check out their water supply. The company, or government,
> doesn't have to pay anyone for services anymore. But even better, this
> kit is so much more advanced than other water testing systems, that it
> can detect viruses or other potentials for disease as soon as they enter
> the water. It's a cheaper, yet more advanced, way of preventing the
> widespread diseases that plague third-world countries. We have an
> enormous market for this kit. We have orders for it already, so revenues
> from the investment are going to be realized very quickly.

I had tape-recorded both his first speech and his second, simpler, explanation. We played them back.

"What was the difference?" I asked.

"The first time I sound like I'm giving a lecture," he said. "In the second I sound like I'm just telling you what the idea is, what you need to know to get interested."

Yahron ended up shortening his presentation to a single page of notes. He practiced with me. And I began to interrupt him, ask questions as he talked—getting him to *dialogue*. At first it bothered him, because he was still thinking that his task was to tell me all the facts as he had arranged them. But eventually he discovered that he didn't need to persuade me of his expertise, he needed to persuade me of the value of the product.

He stopped using multisyllable words just to convince me of his skill in English. He stopped lecturing me. Instead, he found creative new ways of describing the product, such as:

It's like a subway card, or a telephone credit card.

He outlined his presentation by beginning in the middle and listing his most important points on a single sheet of paper. He wanted to get me to understand the value of his product and how it opened up potential markets that seemed logistically unapproachable before. He was prepared to dialogue—to seek and get a response after making each point. He knew, too, that if he structured his presentation as a give-and-take, not a reading of a script, he would get questions on each point.

Then he planned how he would get an immediate response with his beginning. The result, in brief outline form, looked like the following.

BEGINNING

Response-getter:

Mr. Nelson, if I could show you a risk-free way of moving your company into the third-world market, would you be interested? [Mr. Nelson says, "Yes, I'm very interested."]

Yahron's persuasion aim: To win his listeners' company as partners in the new business venture.

MIDDLE

Yahron's persuasion strategy: To structure his presentation topically, presenting each argument for the joint venture, then support it with facts and figures.

Here's how the kit works:

- Describe—it's like a little laboratory in a lunch box.
- Customer pays at time of order—up front.
- No need to bill for services—no collection problems.
- Developing and war-torn areas in need—potential use by military as well as relief branches of governments.

What we offer as a partner:

- Who we are: a global company with a track record in new technology ventures.
- We have developed relationships to new markets in Africa and India.

Your benefits:

- You'll get profits up front.
- You'll develop a new area of business.
- You'll broaden your customer base to include new governments in emerging economies, as well as international relief agencies.

"We want you to join us."

END

Mr. Nelson, together we can pioneer an advanced technology, and open up new markets for our companies. And we can do this without the usual risks associated with third-world ventures. I want to bring you and your associates, and the officers of my company, together to discuss this further. Is there a time when we can meet?

This short outline gave Yahron just the amount of insurance he needed to go into a meeting confident that he would make all his basic points.

By practicing out loud with me, he realized that his simple, everyday language was clearer than the language he had used in his first, written essay.

Most important, when Yahron put his concentration on making me understand, rather than proving his own expertise, his fear subsided. His attention went away from himself and onto me, as he sought to persuade me of the value of his product. As he talked, he concentrated on being clear, seeing if I got his points, making me understand the potential of a partnership.

After the meeting, Yahron reported back to me on how it went. He was very happy with the results: "I speak no more than three or four sentences now. That's it. Then they start asking questions, right away. From there it is very simple. I can make my points as we talk. It's a good product and I know it and they know it. I feel confident now, even relaxed sometimes!"

ELEANOR'S COMPELLING EXAMPLE OF FEARLESS SPEAKING
Speak Up and Save Your Life

Eleanor is the editor of a health care magazine. She is also a perfectionist. After hearing this story about her friend, she felt strongly about the need to be prepared for what might happen during a hospital stay.

When she gave this speech in class, she had it written out word for word. It lacked spontaneity and lost some of its potency because of this. After her first rendition, I asked her to write an outline of the structure and its major points, then using that as a guide, tell us this true story of a writer friend of hers. She had to think while she was talking. Her delivery became *real*. The listeners responded.

BEGINNING

Response-getter:

> How many saw the movie *Terms of Endearment*, when Shirley MacLaine refused to be cowed by the hospital staff when she knew what needed to be done?
>
> That scene provides a good role model for us all.
>
> Here's what happened to a friend of mine. It's not a pleasant story. It's not for the squeamish.

Eleanor's persuasion aim:

> But it must be told, because it illustrates how hospitals can be dangerous to your health—if you don't speak up, ask for information, and

question procedures that don't make sense to you. This story will teach you what you must do if you want to leave the hospital in better shape than when you went in.

MIDDLE

Eleanor's persuasion strategy: To support her argument by recounting her friend's hospital experience in narrative form, allowing it to unfold like a story and build to a climax.

My friend is a well-known, respected medical journalist, recently retired from a major network. He gave daily television reports on health and medicine. He writes a monthly column for a national publication on health.

He is obviously someone well informed, up-to-date, familiar with the medical system. Yet, as a patient, he got into physical danger in the hospital. It was a potentially life-threatening situation. That frightens me. If it could happen to him—with all his resources and knowledge—what does that mean for the rest of us?

It means we can learn from his mistake.

So here is what happened:

My friend was admitted to a hospital [a major teaching hospital in New York] for treatment on an irregular heartbeat.

He also had a troublesome urinary sphincter that would spasm and clamp down. But he had been taking some pills at home for that problem, and it was under control.

He only took two of these pills with him to the hospital, assuming the doctors there would give him whatever he needed. But he needed to take the pills regularly, and when he ran out it was late at night and the nurses would not do anything without doctor's orders.

My friend's sphincter closed at midnight. No doctors were available to write a prescription. He complained. A resident came by and talked to the nurse, who pointed to a bag partly filled with urine. If the resident had spoken to my friend, however, he would have learned that the urine had been released prior to running out of the drug.

The next four to five hours were a horror. My friend suffered excruciating pain. He could not get his urologist on the phone. He complained to the nurse, to no avail. Finally, at 7 A.M., a nurse took pity on my friend and put him in a warm sitz bath to try to relax his sphincter. But it didn't help.

At 8 A.M. one of my friend's doctors finally did come around, took one look at my friend, and yelled for a urological resident. The resident inserted a catheter and released over a quart of urine.

My friend's bladder could have burst, the urine could have backed up into his kidneys, creating a life-threatening situation.

END

So what was my friend's mistake?

He was too passive, too polite.

You need an advocate to stay on top of things, to make sure what is supposed to happen does happen.

My friend's advice: "Yell and scream . . . and loudly."

Some people are shy because they fear staff retribution.

Don't. A hospital is a bureaucracy. Things move slowly. Mistakes can happen.

Have an advocate. Demand information. Question procedures. Don't abdicate your power.

If you do, it could cost you your life! And in some unfortunate situations could lead to a protracted, undignified, even painful death.

When you have prepared a talk or presentation that springs from your intelligence and belief, and you follow the steps of this program . . .

- experiencing your voice,
- getting response and developing a structure,
- dialoguing,
- being creative, and
- using persuasion,

. . . delivery of what you say is more effective. Speaking your message becomes easy to do. It also achieves success. It makes you fearless.

Assignment Five

Give an 8- to 10-minute talk to a group of eight or more people. Your purpose is to persuade them to take a specific action.

1. Choose a topic you believe in and want to convince others to believe in, too. Decide how you want to affect your listeners, what action you want them to take.

2. Select your response-getter—a provocative question, a startling exhibit, a moving anecdote.

3. Structure your talk as always, beginning in the middle, then the conclusion, then the opening.

4. Choose your audience, and answer this question: What do I want these people to do after they've heard what I have to say?

5. Each of your points in the body of your talk should be an argument for whatever you are trying to persuade your listeners to do.

6. Support each point with evidence—warnings, reasons, statistical data, personal experience, stories of the experiences of others, historical data.

7. Do whatever research is necessary to make your case.

8. Practice with a tape recorder.

9. Give the presentation, and tape it.

10. Listen to the tape, and fill out the Self-Critique Questionnaire.

11. Do Voice Exercise #5 (see Appendix A). Begin with Voice Exercises #1 through #4.

Self-Critique Questionnaire for Step Five

▶ What did I discover about the way I organized my argument? (Too few points, too many? Did they follow sequentially?)

▶ What would I add or change to make it more effective?

▶ What seemed to move the audience most?

▶ How did this speech change my own thinking about myself as a speaker?

SCHEDULE FOR WORKSHOP #5

1. Do Voice Exercises #1, #2, #3, #4, and #5 as a group.

2. Go around the room and have each person give his or her prepared speech to the entire group.

3. After everyone has finished, take a few minutes and answer your Self-Critique Questionnaire for Step Five, and share your answers with the group.

4. Read through Assignment Six together.

5. *Homework:* Read Step Six and prepare to do Assignment Six at the next meeting.

▼

Achieve Your Higher Objective

*What lies behind us and what lies
before us are tiny matters,
compared to what lies within us.*

RALPH WALDO EMERSON

In Step Five, you used your communication skills to persuade some-one to take an action. In Step Six, you'll take that process one step further: You'll identify your higher objective, make it the defining goal of your presentation.

That higher objective explains *why* you are asking your listeners to do whatever you are asking them to do. And that *why* is based in your values, your beliefs, your sense of what is right and true.

This step, Achieve Your Higher Objective, is a bridge to Step Seven, Give the Gift of Your Conviction. In that step, you will explore the *because* of your values, which have their roots in your own experience.

So you see how the process of persuasion—asking someone to take an action—can acquire a much deeper sense of mission. In Step Six, you are seeking to transform your listeners in some way—to influence their perceptions and ultimately their behavior. When that is your focus, your fear evaporates because you are involved in something that engulfs you, is meaningful to you, that has deep value for you.

Persuasion—*What*

Objective—*Why*

Conviction—*Because*

What Matters to You?

Before you can speak from the heart—from a position of passion and personal knowledge—you need to know where you stand. What really does matter to you?

Most people, I think, would answer: "Family and friends. Good health. Financial security. World peace."

We put the higher value on "heart" matters, the relationships and connections that are heartfelt: family, religion, country, living worthwhile lives. But I'd like you to be even more specific. Really zero in on what inspires you, what motivates you. The following three people and what inspires them are interesting examples.

Ahmet Ertegun, the urbane, sophisticated, yet down-to-earth, founder and chairman of Atlantic Records, is known and respected throughout the music industry for his lifelong commitment to American jazz and blues. He is a pioneer in bringing rare music into the mainstream. In the 1950s, he openly defied prevailing racial prejudices and opened the door to Ray Charles and many other successful minority artists. On a CBS *Sunday Morning* show, Ertegun told correspondent Ed Bradley he still prefers what he calls the real music of the people—hillbilly and the blues—and now he loves rap music as much as he loved blues in the early days. Ertegun said, "I think rap has taken the place of blues as the expression of Black people. I don't think Americans should be shocked at the music as much as they should be shocked at what causes people to say some of the things they say in records."

Architectural historian Victoria Newhouse, author of *Towards a New Museum* (The Monacelli Press, 1998), spent several years visiting new museums in the United States and in Europe. Struck by the disparity between these buildings, she decided to try and describe why some new museum buildings work, while others fail, in a way that would help future clients and architects.

Her main concern is that architecture and art complement one another. To achieve this, she feels that museum buildings must be treated with the same respect as the art they contain. This is often not the case, especially for additions, as, for example, New York's Solomon Guggenheim Museum, where Frank Lloyd Wright's masterpiece has been compromised by a 10-story tower. Indignation about this kind of design desecration together with indifference to changing a museum's personality—as does the Louvre's new airport-like entrance lobby under I.M. Pei's pyramid—impassion her discussion.

Robin Groth is an Emmy-award-winning television journalist. Most recently, Robin joined CNN as a correspondent and producer. For almost a decade, she has reported on children's health care for World Vision, an international relief organization traveling to Africa, Brazil, Romania, and Bangladesh. This year she asked World Vision to help her find the child she had sponsored to feed, clothe, and educate for eight years. When Kelebogile walked through the World Vision door of a mud hut in a village in Botswana, she smiled at Robin, holding a tattered photograph Robin had sent her eight years ago. Robin's eyes brimmed over with joyous tears.

They became acquainted, then they spent the afternoon shopping. Robin is as passionate about this part of her life as she is about her broadcasting career. She cares about the world's children and inspires others to join in her enthusiasm. I look forward to her holiday card each year to see which country she has traveled to, to bring solace, nurturing, and life to a child.

Each of these people enjoys a singular devotion to a personal and professional passion. Yours may be more varied and less intense. But you *do* care. You *do* have values and cherish them. You just need to dig into yourself and bring your values to the fore.

What causes seem most compelling to you? The environment? Saving the rain forests? Fighting racism and anti-Semitism?

What social, medical, and economic problems worry you the most? Health care delivery? Breast cancer research? Income tax reform? Education?

If you won millions in the lottery and could give a large donation to any cause or charity, which one would you choose? Why?

Is the world a better place than it was 10, 20, 30 years ago? If you could live in any other time period, which one would you choose? Why?

Is the company you work for on the right track? Can the new project you will be describing in your presentation help keep it that way? How important is it that everyone understand this project?

Should we require that children wear uniforms in our schools? Is it really an economic hardship for some parents, or more of a blessing for many?

What *really* pushes your button? Drives you up the wall? What obvious solutions to chronic problems are we overlooking?

The list of questions could go on and on. You can think of dozens of your own and answer them.

As a speaker, most of the time, you will have at least some flexibility in choosing your subject. Even if the topic is a work assignment, you can still try to make your own life's vision play a role in it.

The key is bringing to light your own caring, your own values, your own human essence. Then, having received a response and outlined your presentation, and stated the arguments you deeply believe in, you support them with your own reasoning, experience, and research. You can say what *matters* to you. And when you do that, your passion outweighs your fear.

Career Terror and You

In business speeches, identifying and communicating your higher objective also is a critical component of fearless speaking. Your higher objective in a business setting may simply be to do an outstanding job because you are a professional. Your goal: communicating how valuable a resource you—the whole and real you— really are.

Earlier in this book, I listed career terror as one of the five principal causes of fear of speaking. The numbing fear of career terror that makes business presentations so agonizing for you is the result of many pressures, restrictions, and frustration. Among them:

- The stakes are often high in business presentations. Major accounts are won or lost. Important clients are impressed, or not. Promotions and plum assignments may hinge on the outcome of your presentation.

- You may be newly promoted to a job with much more responsibility and feel immense pressure to turn in a performance that justifies the promotion.

- Your boss is intimidating and you perceive him or her to be disapproving.
- You know that someone in the audience is hostile to you, perhaps rooting for you to fail.
- You are required to follow a prewritten script and adhere to a rigid format.
- You feel obligated to use language that is favored by the company, though it seems forced and stilted to you.
- You are called at 10 P.M. and told you must fly to another city early the next day and preside at a midmorning presentation. You don't feel prepared.
- You're assigned to talk about something you know nothing about. (I'm constantly amazed at how often this happens.)
- You're comfortable with telephone conference calls, then overnight videoconferencing becomes the in-house technology *du jour,* and you feel like you have to give a television performance.
- The unspoken expectation at your company is that everybody has something to say at every one of the many meetings that consume so much of the work week. You feel inadequate—and consequently frightened—because you feel you don't measure up to the competition.
- You are capable, well-prepared, and highly effective in your job, except when you have to stand up behind a lectern and give a speech. In one-on-one and small group situations, you are a leader whose ideas are sought and acted upon. In fact, your ideas are so good, slick colleagues hijack them and present them at meetings, while you fume in silence.

American corporations lead the world in their technological communications skills. The forward-looking company today invests thousands and even millions in state-of-the-art equipment that can place employees who are physically on opposite sides of the globe face to face via satellite.

Meanwhile, many of these companies lag behind in their understanding of *real* communication—the kind that takes place between people.

A client of mine, an international megacorporation, serves as a good example. This corporation spends millions on what it believes to be effective communications. Every presentation, every report, every appearance by anyone at any level to anyone else within the company is researched, studied, written, and rewritten to the max, according to exhaustive policies, rules, and guidelines. Every detail is scrutinized, examined, weighed, and examined again before the final script is approved.

Despite all of this thoroughness and devotion to a perfectionist ideal, the corporation's top executives are at a loss to understand why communications within their walls break down, why their carefully rehearsed presentations fail.

The answer is simply this: The people doing the communicating are discouraged from putting anything of themselves into their speaking chores. The script, so the thinking goes, is so good, the words so well-honed, the factual data so well-sifted and potent, that (1) *everyone* should be able to understand it, and (2) *anyone* should be able to deliver it.

That won't work. And then to compound their confusion, when the execs come looking for help, they imagine the problem can be solved by treating externals: proper eye contact, correct cadence, voice modulation, how far to stand from the microphone, when to turn the lights down. They want to treat a life-threatening disease with cosmetic surgery!

Here's what many of my students from the business world—those who work daily in the white-collar trenches and on the firing line of middle management—tell me about their experience with corporate pressure.

The employees believe they ought to be able to produce (they mean "read aloud") these oral presentations perfectly, making every effort *not* to connect with their listeners. They watch their peers and superiors "get through it beautifully" (they mean "read aloud without faltering") and are saddened to think they themselves "have no gift for this sort of thing."

So everyone is talking—intoning, reciting, silently panicking, praying they won't go blank—and no one is listening.

There is a better way.

MYTHS

I'm better off winging it.

The venerable actress, Ruth Gordon, said it best: "The very best impromptu speeches are the ones written well in advance."

Watch yourself in the mirror.

Why? You don't talk to yourself when you speak, so why look at yourself? Imagine whom you are talking to.

Make eye contact.

Merely looking up from your outline is not making eye contact. Getting a response from people by looking at them is.

Begin with a joke.

Unless you are a comedian, try something a bit safer. There are other, surer ways to make your audience comfortable and get a response. Use one of those.

"He's a natural."

Just because a person has the ability to get up and talk before a group of people does not necessarily make him an effective speaker, and if he is effective, he most likely has prepared over a length of time, gathering creative, pertinent material that matters to him. Then he puts his thoughts in an order that is clear and attention-getting.

You can't change your voice.

Your voice is as unique as your fingerprint. But you can change it by enlarging its scope in range, speaking on different pitches, making it resonant, using different rhythms, ridding yourself of nasality, and clarifying your articulation. It takes training and practice.

How to Achieve *Your* Objective and the Boss's Objective

Public speaking on your job should not be formulaic and uncreative. You can express yourself—serve your own higher objective—within the framework that has been given to you as a corporate speaker. Your goal and their goal do not have to be incompatible.

Look again at the section earlier in this chapter on identifying what matters to you. There you considered those things in your life that you care most about, those cultural or creative pursuits that you know well and love, the cosmic issues that are most compelling to you. You realized, in case you ever doubted it, that you are not an automaton, a statistic, just another head in the head count. You have your own values, your own priorities, your own faith, your own sense of what matters.

Even if the work you do isn't your dream come true, you must have a heart connection to it. It is what you do. You must take pride in it.

It feels good to be a professional, a well-trained authority on something that counts in the corporate scheme of things. If nothing else, your personal objective can be to express that professionalism, that excitement.

That means identifying what is important in the material and communicating it. To focus, as always, on *what* you are saying and *why* you are saying it, *not how.*

Sharon, an economist, expressed the idea very well: "I get panicked when my mind is not engaged, and I'm not engaging anyone else's mind," she said. "But when there's an objective—a point to this meeting, something I really want everyone to know and understand—I get involved and I'm not nervous."

Jacqui Achieves Her Higher Objective—And Overcomes Career Terror

Jacqui loves producing television commercials at the major advertising agency where she has been senior account executive for 14 years.

She loves her family and votes in every election, and the sight of the Statue of Liberty always makes her think of her late Italian grandparents.

But what really lights her fire—what she believes is the true essence of Jacqui—is producing television commercials.

She calls it "sending down some beautiful film." By that she means a rough cut of a commercial, the work of a team she supervised, to be presented to a client. At that point, her job is to preside at the meeting, explaining what the finished product will look like, to generate and sustain the client's enthusiasm, and to be able to anticipate and answer questions.

For her, the producing is easy. The speaking is hard. And at one point, her future seemed to depend more on the speaking than the producing. That's why she came to class.

She felt that she was dull and ineffective at meetings and her proof was alarming: She'd been in charge of one of her firm's biggest accounts, a toiletries manufacturer, for a long time. Yet a new divisional president of the company, having watched her in action at three meetings, told her bosses he didn't want her managing the launch of a new shampoo. Jacqui was devastated, saying, "We're trying to convince the client's senior management that our firm and, specifically, I have the vision, the understanding, the knowledge, the expertise to manage this product launch, not only in the U.S., but around the world. . . . Now this new guy comes in, this divisional president, and based on three meetings . . . the 14 years I demonstrated my capability every day mean nothing. He said I stumbled, and didn't seem like someone he wanted launching his product."

Jacqui faced a frustrating, and all too common, dilemma. Out of the spotlight, she was a dynamo in a very difficult job. In the spotlight, she faltered.

"My job is to manage a large group of creative people and get them to think the same way creatively," she explained. "I love doing that. The responsibility is to set the vision, get their input and modify. Get this large group of people heading in the same direction."

She continued, "What I love is thinking up a strategy and working with the creatives to come up with the magic. Those are good meetings, when we're defining it, shaping it. In fact, they're not like meetings at all. What I find difficult is actually taking someone through the process of how we got there."

Jacqui also echoed some of her fellow students' common complaints about corporate communications and the culture of meetings.

Often, she said, she was given very little time to prepare. On an hour's notice, she'd be asked to speak on something she felt she knew nothing about. Or she'd get a call late at night and find herself on a plane to Cincinnati first thing in the morning, frantically putting together notes for a meeting.

And she was frustrated by what she felt was pressure to conform to corporate language—the buzzwords.

I asked Jacqui how her coworkers—all those creative people on her team—would describe her.

"They would say that I'm confident, that I'm smart, that I'm driven, and that I have a good sense of humor," she replied. "But I'm not like that when I give presentations. I lose my fire. I don't feel I have an identity when I'm in the room, like I'm not real."

Our job, then, was to get the real Jacqui into the room with the bosses and the clients, to let them see her the way she really was.

We began by examining objectives: theirs and hers.

"There are two," she decided. "Theirs, and by extension, mine, is that 'We are the advertising agency you want.' But mine goes farther. It is, 'I am the resource you want.' Taking the objective a step farther: 'I am the resource any complex, creative project of this kind needs. I have the experience and the vision to make it happen. And what I want most, at this moment, is to share that experience and vision with you.' "

Tackling the Seven Step Program, Jacqui learned how to experience the voice that made her so popular with her colleagues and use it to get and keep response from small, friendly audiences; to dialogue with them; to apply to formal presentations the persuasive interpersonal communications skills that served her so well when she was out of the spotlight.

Her higher objective—to communicate "I am the resource you want"—was strong and guided her into giving the gift of her conviction. (This is explained in detail in Step Seven.)

She learned to do what she did in *real* conversations at cocktail and dinner parties: "To kick into who I really am."

And what about the toiletries company's hostile division president, the one who wanted Jacqui off his case?

Jacqui made a decision about her presentations to that client. She asked herself, "Is my objective to turn him around and have him come running up afterward and say, 'You are the answer to my prayer'? Or is my objective to conduct a meeting so that each person goes away stronger, more refreshed, more self-confident in what they know and what I have helped them achieve?"

She chose to focus on the latter. And by all accounts she succeeded with everyone but Mr. Big.

Today, Jacqui has no regrets. She's a top account executive with another agency, applying and reaping the rewards from her fearless speaking.

KATHY'S COMPELLING EXAMPLE OF FEARLESS SPEAKING
Women Talk, We Listen

Kathy Dwyer, president of Revlon Consumer Products USA, gave this speech at the 1998 *Women's Wear Daily* Summit. Kathy does not have a fear of public speaking. Her concern (if any) is to keep the audience from being bored, so she cleverly and creatively uses video and slides of the products she talks about to keep the juices—hers and the audience's—flowing. This is an example of a persuasive presentation motivated by a higher objective. (This version is excerpted from the original.)

Her topic: "Where Women Go, We Will Follow."

BEGINNING

Response-getter:

I'd like to start by taking a quick poll. Take a look at this statement. [Shows slide.] "Where women go, we will follow."

How many people in this audience believe this? If you do, raise your hand. [Many do.] Exactly what I thought. Terrific!

Telling them what she's going to tell them:

For years, we in the cosmetics business have thought that we set trends and women follow our lead. And of course, we do *influence* women's buying patterns. But I maintain that it has worked the other way around for years now—that where women go, we follow. We don't lead them so much as they lead us.

Objective:

I'm going to try to convince you that this is true, in the U.S. market and ultimately in markets around the world . . .

So, whether you agree with my thesis or not, stay with me . . . Hopefully, I'll provoke you to some new thinking and different attitudes about our business. And, more important, I'll share some information that affects everyone in this room personally and economically."

MIDDLE

Women's agenda has changed from winning and acquiring to possibility, personal progress, and exploring. [Show slide: spiritual, mental, physical well-being.] Today, 40 percent of women claim that the most important part of well-being is spiritual well-being.

[Show video of Madonna, the entertainer.] Madonna, from material girl to motherhood. Like the rest of us, Madonna makes her own money, uses her own influence, has power. Part of her power is that she reinvents herself. She demonstrates that success is about moving and changing.

The ability to change is the basis of women's power. It's one of the things that makes us different from men.

[Show slide: male and female brains.] Men use the left brain—math and spatial functions. Women use the right brain—language and relationships. Did you know that the part of the brain that connects the two halves is larger in women? . . . Biology is on our side.

[Show slide: statistics on women working, gaining in income.] By the year 2000, women will earn 85 to 90 percent of what men earn, up from 63 percent in 1980, they will write 80 percent of checks, own 53 percent of stocks, buy 65 percent of all cars.

Research shows that on a scale of 1 to 10, the average woman rates her attractiveness a 7. [Show slide: the number 7.] And that's good enough. [Show slide: Bo Derek.] Remember when everybody felt pressured to be a 10 or to conform to a look?

[Show slide: *How Stella Got Her Groove Back* book cover.] Today, women are claiming their own look and their own fantasies. . . . We also have a new attitude about beauty. . . . Women are not just accepting what they look like, they're accepting who they are. They're recognizing that their differences are advantages—not disadvantages.

Role models [show slide] are Rosie O'Donnell, Whoopi Goldberg, Susan Sarandon. We don't admire these women for reinforcing the status quo—we admire them for being themselves. And for creating their *own* "quo."

More than 6 million women baby boomers will celebrate the "big five-oh" by 2005. The largest, richest generation of women ever. And the first with their own money. [Applause from the audience.]

[Show slide: year 2005—Women 50+—46 million.] These women represent *three times* as much opportunity as the youth market. As an industry, we have certainly paid more than our share of attention to the youth market. Historically, we have underserved the needs of women over 50. That might not be the right strategy for the next 20 years.

[Show slide: color cosmetics growth in dollars and percentages.] When women feel more powerful and have more purchasing power, it's great for the cosmetics business. Women express their sense of self through color cosmetics. . . . Every woman is searching for those products and those moments that help her feel good about herself. That help her get a respite from all the stuff bombarding her and that help her feel connected to what's important.

We in the cosmetics industry talk to her in her own language. And women talk back to us—with dollars. Shopping in new ways and leading us to new products.

END

Whether it's developing multibenefit products that save time in women's busy lives or products geared to all the baby boomers turning 50, I hope I've convinced you that to thrive in the future, we will need to listen to women and take our cues from them.

[Show slide: "Where women go, we will follow."] Yes, women are leading. And if we're smart, we will follow.

Kathy's desire to share her belief in the emerging economic power of mature women, and the impact of that power on the cosmetic business, is an objective that makes her speech compelling and convincing.

Kathy has become a fearless speaker. As she was climbing the ladder of success, her voice was rather tentative. Now it is strong and resonant. It soars above the audience of 800 or 1,000 people. She learned through the years the importance of having a clear, structured outline and the value of a persuasive message with a definite objective. In this speech, Kathy carefully chose her slides and video clips to enhance her message and to get response from the listeners. This is the formula for success.

Assignment Six

Give a 10- to 12-minute talk to at least a dozen people on a subject you care about deeply. Your purpose is not just to persuade your listeners to take a specific action, but to communicate to them your own higher objective.

1. Choose a topic that reflects one of those areas of life that are most important to you—home, family, religion, culture, professionalism, and so on.

2. Identify your higher objective in this presentation.

3. Assess your audience. Who are they? Where do they come from? How are their backgrounds similar to yours? Different?

4. Plan to get a response, and structure your presentation as before—middle first, then the end, then the beginning.

5. As you plan your points, connect your arguments and evidence to your own experience and beliefs. For example, don't just tell why it is so important to vote, tell us why it is so important to you.

6. Tap your creativity to make your points and make your objective live for your listeners.

7. Practice with your tape recorder. Critique yourself.

8. You're on! Go out and give the speech. Record it.

9. Listen to the tape, and answer the questions in the Self-Critique Questionnaire for Step Six.

10. Practice Voice Exercise #6, as well as the five voice exercises preceding it (see Appendix A).

Self-Critique Questionnaire for Step Six

▶ How did my objective help me organize my speech?

▶ What creative tools helped me to persuade my listeners and further my objectives?

▶ How did my objective affect the way I spoke and how I felt while speaking?

▶ Did I have a strong conclusion?

▶ What could I do next time to make it better?

SCHEDULE FOR WORKSHOP #6

1. Do Voice Exercises #1, #2, #3, #4, #5, and #6 as a group.

2. Go around the room and have each person give his or her prepared speech to the entire group.

3. After everyone has finished, take a few minutes and answer your Self-Critique Questionnaire for Step Six, and share your answers with the group.

4. Read through Assignment Seven together. Decide on the order in which you will speak next week. The final speech you give—at the next session—will be the most professional speech you'll give, so when you come in next time, think of it more as a real speaking engagement, rather than just another workshop session.

5. *Homework:* Read Step Seven and prepare to do Assignment Seven at the next meeting.

Note: It's a good idea if everyone brings one or two guests to the final session. That way the group will be large enough and filled with enough "strangers" to make the audience representative of an authentic speaking venue. So prepare your speech for next week, keeping in mind that your audience will consist of a larger, unknown group. You'll be fine.

▼

Give the Gift of Your Conviction

When you are inspired by some great purpose, some extraordinary project, all your thoughts break their bonds: your mind transcends limitations, your consciousness expands in every direction and you find yourself in a new, great, and wonderful world. Dormant forces, faculties, and talents become alive, and you discover yourself to be a greater person by far than you ever dreamed yourself to be.

—PATANJALI

I believe everyone has something special to share. We may not be aware of it, but it is within us. Searching for what we find meaningful brings us a deeper sense of ourselves, an acknowledgment of who we are—particularly, uniquely. Sharing that depth with one person or a group of people helps us experience and believe what we are saying in a wholly new way. Sharing your conviction is the greatest gift you can give.

Yet, when you reveal your deepest beliefs and reactions on a personal level, you allow yourself to be vulnerable. At the same time, you become stronger.

When you express conviction, you:

1. *Speak from the core* of what is meaningful to you, and find acceptance or rejection of your beliefs.

2. *Experience the strength* that comes from that acceptance or rejection.

3. *Move to a higher level* of growth and achievement.

Sometimes, in an effort to stay safe and in control, we shy away from what matters most to us, and we talk formally or impersonally, thinking that will make us sound more professional. But every time you are willing to take a risk and bare your soul in front of an audience—to speak in a prepared way about what really matters to you, even when this is scary and self-exposing—you are transformed as a speaker in a way that carries over to all future speaking occasions.

Your convictions are a gift of respect and caring to your listeners. And when people are spoken to in this manner—not merely spoken *at*—they respond in kind.

Lee Strasberg's "Method" and the Real You

I studied with the great acting teacher, Lee Strasberg, for 11 years. I learned acting techniques from him, and through those techniques I learned about life. I base my Speaking with Conviction Method on two of his famous exercises. Both are designed to help students express what is special in their lives. They are:

- The Private Moment (Being Private in Public)
- The Affective Memory

In the Private Moment exercise, you will learn to allow yourself to take a risk, to make yourself vulnerable, to open yourself up to your listeners. In the Affective Memory exercise, you will pinpoint a specific traumatic experience you may have had, or a pattern of traumatic behavior you might have had, which defined your life. I will show you how these two exercises help you plumb the depths of your conviction.

The Private Moment

In *The Actors Studio* (Collier Books, 1980), the book's author, David Garfield, defines the "private moment":

> The private moment was devised by Strasberg in response to his rereading of Stanislavski's remarks about the actor's needing to be "private in public." Its purpose was to help actors inhibited by the presence of the audience to confront this difficulty and overcome it

by enacting a moment of real privacy in front of people. In private, people do things unself-consciously that they could not do in front of others: they talk to themselves or to plants, hold imaginary dialogues with other people, sing or dance with abandon, give vent to strong emotions, and so on. The actor preparing the exercise was instructed to create sensorially the environment in which he felt securely alone. He was even allowed to bring in some familiar objects from home to flesh out this environment. And then, once he achieved a sense of privacy, he was told to try to recapture the reality of his private behavior—some activity he would stop immediately if someone entered his room—and to allow himself to deal with the particular feelings and sensations that would normally cause him embarrassment if observed by others.

Then, in *Strasberg at the Actor's Studio* (Theatre Communications Group, Inc., 1980), edited by Robert H. Hethmon, Lee Strasberg gives this example of the Private Moment exercise, drawn from the experience of one of his students:

> She brought in a Victrola and a Turkish record she had once used in an exercise. Then she did just a moment of being by herself. She was lying in bed in her room all alone, because she only does this when she's by herself and in a mood everybody gets into sometimes. Then she put on the Turkish music and started to dance. You have never seen such abandon as this girl had on the stage. It was what I call hot dancing, and it was exciting, thrilling, shocking in the sense that you just didn't think of this kind of thing with that girl. She hadn't seemed that kind of girl.
>
> It acted like a tonic. From then on her work changed. There was a real break in the continuity of her acting. Her voice began to alter. Many more vocal colors began to come through. She began really to think on stage, and thinking began to take possession of her. We encouraged her to pick scenes in which something like this private moment could be done, and we began to get from her an ease and a fullness of response, and finally in one scene she was going along, going along, and—wham!—she burst out as in the Private Moment exercise. Thus we were able to counter her long-induced habits of not expressing as fully as she could what in fact she did feel.

Now you may be thinking, "What does dancing to Turkish music have to do with giving a report to my board of directors or my boss, or trying to achieve my speaking potential?" Let me explain.

What I am suggesting is that you think about something you would like to do, something you consider your wildest dream—conduct the New York Philharmonic, for instance, or be one of those amazing acrobatic performers in Cirque du Soleil, or ski jump to an Olympic gold medal. Or imagine a moment of accomplishment you remember as an exquisite moment of happiness in your life—the way you felt when you were accepted to the school of your choice, won the tennis tournament, or received the promotion you waited for so long.

Personally, I've always wanted to be like Julie Andrews in *My Fair Lady*. And I used that daydream to create my favorite Private Moment.

When I read that Andrews would make a guest appearance on television, I taped the show, hoping she would sing "I Could Have Danced All Night." To my delight, she did.

When no one but my dog Inka was around, I played the tape and sang along with Julie Andrews. Inka was my audience, and I tried to get her to move in rhythm with me. I imagined playing Eliza Doolittle on Broadway to an enthusiastic audience—visualizing other characters in the show—singing out with fullness and in sweet tones. At times I couldn't quite make the high notes; Julie Andrews need not fear competition from me. Still, I had a grand time. It was good to experience my sound and my body moving.

My Eliza Doolittle Moment has served me well (yes, even teachers need them). I use it to prepare for a time of both pleasure and stress in any teacher's life—the first day of class.

How to Find and Use Your Private Moment

Finding, experiencing, and applying your Private Moment is a structured process. If all you do is mull it over while you drive or ride the subway or cook, and then store it away, it won't do you much good. You must act it out. Experience it with your senses and then you will be able to access it when you need it.

Here's how:

1. Choose your favorite Private Moment from among your wild dreams and fantasies. Or think of something you have always been afraid to share with other people.

2. Act it out in privacy. Call upon your senses of sight, sound, taste, touch, and smell. Use music, lights, props if you like. When you make reference to the soft glow of a lamp, really try to see it, or when you feel the rug under your feet, try to recall its stiffness or its plushness. Use your senses.

3. Then choose a friend—better yet, a group—and tell them your dream or nightmare. As you experience it, describe it in detail. Use your words to provide a sensory experience for your audience. Be as specific as you can.

The aftereffect of this exercise will be a wonderful feeling of independence, elation, accomplishment. You've just achieved a high level of self-realization. Let that feeling seep into your body.

Then, when the time comes to speak in public, as you sit on the dais waiting to be called, or as you walk to the lectern, recall the sensory awareness you felt when you expressed yourself with abandon and depth. It will just take a second to rev up your senses of sight, sound, taste, touch, and smell.

That experience will carry over into your presentation at work or in the community. It will help you speak with conviction.

You may think there is no connection between dancing as prima ballerina in *Swan Lake* or pitching a no-hitter for the Yankees and the need for qualified teachers in the education system. But there is.

Here's how the Private Moment benefited some of my students:

• Ray, a buyer for a major department store, told us his secret fantasy was to be a game show host. With the class as his audience, Ray improvised a mock game show with all its razzle-dazzle. Not long after that, Ray and his partner attended a Gay Rights March in Washington. Remembering the sensations he felt during his Private Moment and the confidence it gave him, he told us later, enabled him to speak out about the rally—something he would not have been able to do before.

• Cynthia, a widowed social worker, gave us a demonstration of T'ai Chi, in all its slow balletic grace. She had practiced it in private for years, but never performed it in front of other people. Cynthia, who had never taken such a risk before, put her heart and soul into the demonstration. Later, she told us the release she felt enabled her to talk publicly for the first time about her husband's death.

- Stan, an advertising executive constantly under stress to meet deadlines, always dreamed of driving a dogsled in the fabled Iditarod race across the frozen wilderness of Alaska. Not only did he imagine it, he actually lived it: He went to Alaska and drove a team of dogs in the race. He told us he took that vigorous trek as an opportunity to practice projecting his voice exercises. Instead of reciting numbers and poetry while pulling in his abdomen and diaphragm, however, he commanded, "Mush! Mush!" In times of stress now, Stan recalls the exhilaration he felt while skimming along the frozen trail and the wonderful sound of his own voice filling the frosty air.

When you take a risk and realize that people accept you as you are, you are transformed. When people respond positively to what you think is your silliest or most vulnerable behavior, you are no longer afraid of making a fool of yourself or of baring your soul.

Affective Memory

The Private Moment and the Affective Memory are similar in their use of sensory recall to get to a deep place in a person. But, unlike the Private Moment, the Affective Memory exercise isn't a fantasy. It's a remembrance of something very real that happened to you—a time of anguish, loss, or betrayal. Affective Memory is an exercise that helps you plug into what you care about on a visceral level. And what you care about is connected to what you have conviction about.

Doing this exercise helps you fuel your conviction and connects you with yourself and your audience. When you speak from deep conviction, you speak fearlessly.

A word of caution: *Please understand that, even though this exercise is similar to techniques used by professional therapists, it is not intended here as a substitute for therapy. Victims of physical abuse and other serious trauma should seek medical treatment. I'll say more about this in Appendix B and recommend places to go for help.*

How to Find and Use Your Affective Memory

Like finding your Private Moment, identifying and experiencing your Affective Memory can't be done while you're doing something else. Make time for it, concentrate on it, and follow these steps:

1. Pick a quiet place where you can be alone and not be disturbed. Sit in a chair and do your relaxation exercises to get rid of all tension. Keep your eyes closed.

2. Think back to a time in your life when something happened that caused you anguish. Pick an experience that has a deep resonance in your body.

3. Gradually, start to recall out loud to yourself one sensory experience after another. Just tell the memory you have of the *sensations* you felt—sights, sounds, tastes, touches, smells. You don't even have to speak in complete sentences. Phrases or simple word associations often are best. Don't tell the circumstances of the event or recite a narrative, just describe the sensations you felt at the time. What objects were in the room? Do you remember a particular smell? Certain sounds? Try to recreate the event in your imagination—to live through it again. The cumulative effect of all these sensory realizations may provoke an emotional reaction in you.

You can do this exercise alone, but if you feel able and ready to do it in front of friends or a class, all the better. No one can require you to reveal your deep feelings about yourself unless you want to. The important part of the exercise is the experience of remembering the sensory sensations. That will give you the fuel you need to talk about what really matters to you.

Sharing your Affective Memory with a teacher, a therapist, a member of the clergy, or someone else you trust completely helps you understand and feel compassion for yourself.

Regardless of whether you choose to verbally share your Affective Memory with someone, do write it down in your notebook. Record all the details, every sensory experience. Writing it down gives you a mastery of it and helps cement the sensations in your mind.

What if you can't think of a specific emotional moment? Recall, instead, a pattern of treatment that made you feel diminished, sad, angry, or frustrated. For example, did your teachers consistently misunderstand you, making you feel lazy and stupid when in fact you had a special need that cried out for attention? Were you shamed by other children because you were different from them or because of your appearance, your race, your religion? Were you constantly put down by a parent or other adult authority figure? The painful sensory experiences of negative treatment over a period of time can be recalled, too.

How, then, do you apply the Affective Memory to fearless speaking? The same way you apply the Private Moment: You access it, remember it, think about it when it is time to speak in public.

When you have a major presentation to give that requires strong belief—you need to persuade an audience, advocate a cause, examine a problem and advance a solution, or just seek support for a point of view—accessing your Affective Memory will help you speak from a base of deep personal conviction.

I did this exercise for the first time in one of Lee Strasberg's classes. I chose a time-pressured good-bye to my father at the train station as he was leaving for Los Angeles. Although there was great tension in our lives, I was unaware that he was leaving my mother, my brothers, and me in a separation attempt. I never saw my father alive again.

But, in the exercise, I didn't tell any of that. Instead, I stuck to what I was sensing—the smell of the trains and my heart pounding, running to the train, my father's red-rimmed eyes. As I recounted the sensory responses, a great well of emotion came to the surface.

I had no idea what to expect when I started the exercise. But as I experienced one sensation after another, I began crying uncontrollably. I was an exhausted heap of a person devastated by a past trauma.

The results of this were twofold.

First, as an actress, I would be able to call up this experience during a scene of a play when I wanted and needed to help bring passion and immediacy to that moment. It then became a real moment for me. Consequently, the other actors and the audience, unknowingly, experienced a "real" moment, too.

Second, I acquired a deeper understanding of myself, my desires, and my fears. I defined my life. I learned why I have a passion to accomplish things before "missing the train." This has led me to become perfectionistic, which can be a problem. At the same time, I'm glad that it has motivated me to excel.

Because Strasberg's techniques worked so well for me, I adapted them for my teaching and have used my own variation of them for many years. I ask students to reveal to the class private moments and personal experiences that affected them and shaped their lives, to make themselves vulnerable and experience the positive feedback they receive.

Here are the stories of two students who incorporated the spirit and meaning of the Private Moment and Affective Memory into their preparation and delivery of a speech. Like them, once you master these two exercises, you will find that you will use them to help you define what really matters to you. That conviction will help make you a fearless speaker.

The first story is about a man who *risked being private in public* and then went on to do a professional speech with conviction.

An Unexpected Private Moment

Sam Young was born in Korea. He is a lawyer. Physically he is tall, strong, and vigorous. He took my class at the New School to learn how to overcome his fear of speaking before a judge and before his peers. He also wanted to learn how to make presentations to prospective investors in his portfolio management work, as well as to learn how to speak up and ask questions in classes. "I have no fear of speaking one-on-one," he said, "but when there are three or five, fifty or a hundred people in a room, especially prospective investors, I am fearful."

Sam gave the following speech in class in response to the assignment: *Describe your most moving or most favorite weekend.* This turned out to be a very private moment.

> Do you think a married man who can go through a separation . . . has the peace of mind to think about his favorite weekend? Is such luck and luxury allowed when he is also separated from his kids? It's frankly odd. I did have one weekend this past summer which I will treasure as my favorite weekend for a long time. I had a heartbreaking experience that involved my daughter who is not far away from my heart.

My kids came from Korea on July 17th which was a Saturday. I hadn't seen them for five months. I could hardly wait to see their little faces once they left North Korea. Both with a pair of China black eyes. One just turned four that day and one was eighteen months old. My heart throbbed as I anxiously paced up and down the international hallway at Kennedy Airport. My eyes fixed on the big moving doors which swung open once in a while to allow the arriving passengers to successfully negotiate with customs.

Although it had been some time since I had seen my kids, I knew my son would have no problem recognizing me. I also knew his first question would be, "What did you get me for my birthday?" To which I would reply, "A birthday card," and let him grumble until he discovered his shiny, black Batmobile parked in his bedroom. I was not so sure about my daughter. In fact, I was not so sure if she would remember me at all. After all, she was only eighteen months old and I had not been in her physical, visual world more than half of her lifetime. Whenever I called my two kids on the phone, my daughter, who cannot talk, could blow out a whisper, "Abba," which means *daddy* in Korean. And that only after repeated coaching by her mother. She didn't know what *abba* meant. It was a sound she was supposed to make while holding the receiver after hearing an agitated man's voice on the other end who was desperately trying to communicate his affection for her.

The customs door swung open, and I took a peek through the opening. My son spotted me and yelled out, "Abba!" And he asked me the question I expected and was gone after hearing my reply. His mother was holding my daughter's hand, and I gave my right hand to Chris . . . and I immediately turned my attention to my daughter. She looked like a doll. I knelt down and extended my arms, waiting for her. . . . She let me pick her up and carry her in my arms, but all the while her eyes would never leave her mother for a moment. I tried to put her head against my chest so she could hear my heartbeat, and I said "Abba" in her ear. While she was still an infant, whenever she was fighting the world, she cried. I used to put her head sideways against my chest so that she could not only hear my heart beating, but also feel it. That used to calm her down. But now, that didn't seem to work either. My own daughter was not able to recognize me. I was frustrated and getting angry at my wife who I thought was responsible for this temporary amnesia. During our drive home, I gave occasional glances at my daughter through the rearview mirror. She would look at me in the mirror one moment and then hastily look away as our eyes met. She was not sure.

We arrived home. The kids' grandparents and cousins were all assembled to stage a surprise party for my son. The door of my apartment opened and eight or so faces all shouted, "Surprise!" as we all walked in. My son was excited to find so many faces waiting for him. My daughter was scared to find so many faces surrounding her at once. I noticed she quit looking around and she started crying. She was trying to wiggle herself out of my arms and reach out to her mother who was still a little defensive about the way my little daughter was reacting to the situation. I had to seize the moment. I turned her head around so that she would have to face me. I gave her the most gentle and reassuring look I could think of, and gently put her head against my chest and held her in that position for a while. I wanted her to hear and feel my heartbeat, hoping that she would remember the heartbeat. I whispered "Abba" into her ear.

Suddenly, she stopped crying and pressed her ear against my chest. She then looked up at me. She again pressed her ear against my chest, listened to my heartbeat some more, and then looked up at me again. Her eyes became progressively perky, her gaze more searching and meaningful. Then she pressed her ear against my chest for some more. I felt the pressure against my chest becoming stronger and surer. Suddenly, she squeezed my neck with her arms and said, "Abba, Abba, Abba." She had remembered and suddenly the beautiful smiling face approached mine and gave me back one small smooch. I thought my eyes were getting a little blurry as I felt a sudden surge of emotion. I squeezed my daughter gently, but tightly, in my arms. At last, my daughter rediscovered me. I was thinking, "Wow, this is powerful." Just as I was thinking it, I heard my son shout, "Wow." It wasn't that my son was moved by what had just happened, he just discovered the Batmobile, which was parked in his bedroom. "Wow, wow," he continued. "Wow," I concurred.

The kids are back in Korea now, and I am, again, separated. But that weekend, when my heartbeat awakened my daughter's memory, will remain as my favorite weekend for a long, long time.

After the speech I asked Sam if he realized how he had involved us and moved us by the story, and his response was something like, "No, I didn't know that I was doing that."

I said, "Couldn't you see the tears in my eyes, let alone Denise using a handkerchief?"

He said, yes, he did see that. But until he gave this speech, he didn't realize the power of sharing his feelings, and convictions with an audience.

This was an enlarging experience for Sam. He spoke from his heart to a group of people and received their respect in return. Every time I've witnessed this process, it has proven to be a strengthening experience for both the person speaking and the listeners.

Since Sam had an upcoming business presentation at work, his eighth and final assignment was to test it on the class. His objective was to sell a group of mutual funds that would yield 20 percent profit to a small group of investors. Minimum investment was $1 million. Sam had to truly believe that the stocks would pay off.

The people in class role-played being the investors. After Sam presented the basic premise of his investment plan, there were questions from the class, a lively discussion, and his answers. Because he had learned he had the power to move people when he spoke from his heart, he was able to speak with a great deal of conviction about the stocks and his plan. Instead of it being an overwhelming situation for him, it became challenging and enjoyable.

Sam's efforts to control his fear of speaking are part of an ongoing process. He now knows how to strengthen his conviction and how to center himself. He knows that he can reach from his core and connect, not only with his daughter, but with the jury, the judge, and investors. Sam knows that other people are as vulnerable as he is and as strong as he is. He has experienced giving and taking in front of other people in class, and he is more able to handle the dialogue of his work life.

You may think that teaching your child of 18 months to recognize and love her father has no connection to selling investments at a 20 percent profit, or speaking to a judge and jury, but it does. All of these efforts are based on strong belief. All are based on taking a risk. All are based on the conviction that you will succeed. That conviction helped Sam Young to overcome his fears of speaking. When Sam revealed his need to connect with his 18-month-old daughter in front of a class at the New School, he had no idea he was doing the Private Moment exercise. He gained a deeper sense of himself and a strength, which he has been able to transfer to his public life. That passion and conviction are now used in his work as a lawyer and a businessman.

The second example is that of a woman who shared her traumatic Affective Memory with me.

Peggy's Use of an Affective Memory

Peggy Lynch teaches writing in a fifth-grade class in a suburb of Detroit. The class includes children with special needs. These children might be ESL (English as a Second Language) students, students with disruptive behavioral problems, or children who are today labeled "learning disabled." Peggy believes strongly that these children should be included in regular classes instead of isolated in special classes. She feels that by becoming part of the regular class community, their self-esteem will improve.

Peggy was scheduled to give a speech to a group of 500 educators in Chicago who wanted to know the benefits of including children with special learning needs in the classroom. She came to me for help because she was afraid to speak in front of that many people.

When I asked Peggy why she was doing this speech, she said, "Because I feel I need to get over my fear of speaking before large groups, and because I want to get out and publicize my book, and also because I fervently believe these children should be included in the classroom."

During the first session I tried to get Peggy *oriented:* to visualize the actual circumstances of the speech, the place, the time, and the nature of it. We talked about the length of the speech; she said they were asking her to speak for 45 minutes and she thought that was too long. She thought that the audience might fall asleep, that the waiters might be rattling the dishes during the luncheon. "That's enough to make anyone nervous, isn't it?" I asked. Peggy agreed.

Step One: Experience Your Voice

Also, at this first session I gave Peggy *voice exercises.* I wanted her to have a sense of the range of her own sound so that she could wipe out that little-girl sound, which her third-grade teacher ridiculed. I taught her how to use her abdomen and diaphragm muscles to project the sound and make it more resonant. I explained to Peggy that these exercises had to be practiced separately, away from the speech that she was giving, but that if she practiced these exercises every day her voice would strengthen and develop, and the sound would then be transferred to her everyday conversation, presentations, and teaching. This is a hard concept for people to accept. It requires a lot of patience, and patience is difficult, because as soon as you learn how the muscles of your body affect your sound, you want to be able to put them into practice; you want to be able to do them all the time. But these muscles need time to be strengthened before they can become automatic.

Step Two: Get a Response and Structure Your Thoughts

At the second session, Peggy practiced getting an immediate response, structuring her speech. I asked her how she would begin the speech and how she would conclude it. Peggy told me that she planned to begin with a poem written by one of her students, a Japanese child named Tamako. Tamako's poem would reflect the themes of her speech and make for a moving beginning. The three main points of the speech would explain her teaching method: ownership, time, and response. She would conclude with a dramatic piece written by Jimmie, a child with criminal tendencies.

Step Three: Establish a Dialogue

For the third session, I suggested that Peggy refine her outline so she would not be buried in the script, reading it. Her response was, "If I don't have every word written down, I'll panic." I assured her she wouldn't because she really knew the material. "I want you to tell it to me, I want you to be more independent. The story is not between you and that piece of paper; it's between you and your listeners."

And Peggy's response was, "But I'll lose my place; that will make me very nervous."

I assured her that she would not lose her place and that if she did, all she had to do was to glance down at her paper and find her place. I told her that as a listener I had enough to think about during a pause and that actually it would be a very good thing for her to pause because then I would be able to use that moment to digest what she had told me.

In this way the speech would become more of a dialogue than a monologue. This helped Peggy talk to me in a more direct way, and I was able to respond to her with "Uh-huh," or "Yes," or "That's great," or by the look in my eye or by the smile on my face, or by the feeling of compassion that I gave back to her for what she gave to me. At this stage, the response she received from me was the key to moving Peggy away from her fears and toward the goal of expressing her conviction. I tried to make her realize she would be getting a response from her audience. In essence, there would be a give-and-take.

Step Four: Tap Your Creativity

At the fourth session, the process became an enlivened one; Peggy was living through it, and I was living through it. Peggy asked, "Aren't you bored? You've heard this so many times." And my response always was, "I couldn't be standing here for 45 minutes reacting to you if I was bored." By this time, Peggy was standing up behind the lectern, and I was using the video camera to record and play back portions for her to see for herself. She began to believe me, and she began to realize that my responses were not manufactured, that they were real, just as what she was giving me was real. It was vibrant. It was active, and we lived this experience together each time she practiced it in front of me.

During the fourth session, Peggy planned on further enlivening her address with creativity by quoting from her students' writings and showing slides of pictures of their notebooks. The development of their language and their sense of belonging ensured the audience's response.

Also at the fourth session, Peggy marked her script for the key words and told the stories her students wrote. I pointed out that she could use humor because the poem that Tamako wrote had elements of Gertrude Stein in it—"Pigeons on the grass, alas," and the like— and she said, "Oh, if only I could. Because I have a sense of humor, you know, it just doesn't come across." We both laughed. Her creativity was awakened and, indeed, she did incorporate the humor.

Step Five: Learn to Persuade

For her fifth session, Peggy prepared the speech with a strong persuasive purpose. Her aim was to get the 500 teachers to agree with her that the children they taught should be included in the classroom, not tutored privately outside of the classroom. She knew it wouldn't be easy.

"There are administrators and teachers who don't agree with this," she told me. "Actually, a lot of teachers feel, 'get these kids with all the learning problems out of my classroom. Keep them with special teachers so I am not responsible for them.' I wanted to show what these kids can do in a regular classroom, how creative they can be."

Step Six: Achieve Your Higher Objective

At the sixth session, Peggy solidified the objective of her speech. Her mission was to convince the 500 teachers in the audience that special children with disabilities belong in the classroom with other children. She knew what she wanted to accomplish from the start. But here she literally *said* it, and she said it with belief and clarity. "I fervently believe these children should be included in the classroom."

Step Seven: Give the Gift of Your Conviction

But how was I going to help Peggy get the fervor and belief so vital to her delivery so that she could let go of reading it word for word and have self-confidence? At the seventh session, I asked Peggy to tell me what it was that gave her the desire to be a teacher. "Did anything special happen to you growing up that made you love the profession, or feel the need to give back to children what you as a child experienced?"

She replied, "Quite the contrary. I went through hell as a student when I was a kid."

Then Peggy sighed and confided in me:

> You know, I was a very quiet child. I barely raised my hand in class to say anything. I was small and skinny, not very sure of myself. I had a teacher who kind of made fun of my voice. It was high-pitched and

soft. She called me baby doll, which made some of the kids laugh. That hurt me. I became embarrassed to speak in class and from then on rarely did.

I remember that my mother told me that when I was two and a half she took me to see Santa Claus and I sat on his lap and I was so frightened of the whole experience that I stopped talking—for 6 months. They took me to hospitals. They took me all over because no one could figure out why I stopped talking. I don't know whether they had to treat me with some kind of drug or something for me to start talking again.

But it even frightened the doctors. They thought "Oh, my God, is she brain damaged?" I had been talking like crazy up to that time, because I was the first born.

Then in middle school or junior high, I did not talk because I was terrified of certain teachers, who would yell and scream and if you didn't say the right answers they would humiliate you. I think the baby doll voice at that time went along with "if you were a girl, you should be dumb and cute and talk like that: a baby doll."

But entering adolescence, I had male teachers who yelled. I was frightened to death. I would never raise my hand. In fact, I was so frightened most of the time I thought I was going to throw up. It's amazing that I ended up teaching.

My mother wanted me to succeed and get good grades at school, but in terms of nurturing, there wasn't much. She never understood how terrified I was to speak in class. She just said, "Oh you can do it."

There was trauma there somewhere (it wasn't just one teacher) and it continued. And to this day, I'm nervous standing up to talk in front of a group. So the fact that I am speaking up in conferences and now exposing myself to these situations means that I really do want to overcome my fear of speaking. But this keynote speech . . .

. . . and then she let out a sound like "Uhhhhhh!"—a sound of terror.

I tried to calm her. "You don't have to worry, Peggy, you're going to be fine. One, you've got a brain, and two, you really care."

When Peggy described to me her difficulty in speaking as she was growing up, she was doing a version of an Affective Memory. She didn't sit in her own room and recall the traumatic incident. Instead, she used her five senses to tell me of the several painful experiences she had growing up and trying to express herself. That opened the door and explained why she had such great rapport with her students. She empathized with them and their problems. She herself suffered in the classroom, and now she wanted to help other children succeed in the classroom. Though at first Peggy was reticent about accepting the connection, as we worked through the steps of the program, she began to believe in the link between what she suffered as a child and what she sees these children suffering. This link gave her more authority in her conviction.

Besides the motivation she had for selling books, I could see that she really cared about the children she taught and believed in her method of teaching. She was convinced that these special children should be taught in the classroom with the other children. Her objective was to persuade each and every person that this was the best and only way to go.

During the seventh session when Peggy practiced conviction, she became truly performance-ready. Peggy had gone through the Seven Steps of the program, including the Affective Memory. When she began to practice out loud, she incorporated the visuals and spoke to the imagined audience with conviction. She began reading the speech. After a few minutes I asked her to *talk* the speech to me, which she did, rather hesitantly, but she got through it. That reinforced her ownership of her words.

As the date of Peggy's speech approached, her fears about the technical aspects of the event took on more importance. She had stopped worrying about her fear of speaking and now wanted to ensure the success of the presentation itself. She began to take charge. She started talking about the man who was arranging this program and the conversations that she had with him. It was supposed to be a luncheon speech, and she was to speak while dessert was being served. We practiced using props at the fourth session (creativity)—slides of the children's drawings—that gave a sense of the beauty, excitement, and growth of these children under her tutelage. I suggested that she get as many of the technicalities cleared up and out of the way as possible over the phone, before she arrived. Then the evening she arrived, she should see the room she would be speaking in and how people were going to be seated, try the microphones, make sure the slides worked, and so on. If not then, she should do so early the next morning.

Dress Rehearsal

The eighth session was a dress rehearsal. We practiced the speech from start to finish and went over the particulars, including what Peggy planned to wear, choosing her slides, imagining the setting, *all* preparations—even having books ready to be signed after the speech, possible interruptions during the speech, questions that might be asked, and having a glass of water handy, but most important, getting Peggy to talk rather than read, and to believe in what she was saying. I videotaped that run-through and played it back. We analyzed it, noting positive aspects as well as what needed fine-tuning. With a memo from me of what to focus on, Peggy was launched.

Peggy called me from Chicago after she gave the speech. She couldn't wait to get back to Detroit to tell me how it went. "First of all," she said, "would you believe the night before I was to give the speech, Fred asked me to cut my speech to thirty minutes, and I said no; if I do that, I am going to have to leave out the story of John, the kid who has criminal tendencies." She said, "I won't do it; you asked me for a forty-five minute speech and here it is." And then she said, "Lilyan, imagine me fighting to have more time to speak rather than less time; a year ago I wouldn't have done that, I would have been glad to cut half of my speech or just to speak for five minutes. I insisted on it and I kept it in because it was such an important part of my speech." Her conviction about teaching had truly overcome her fear of speaking.

Peggy was extremely excited and happy that she had controlled her fear of speaking, that she had accomplished something that was so vital to her life and work. She confided to me in her sweet, charming, elf-like way, "Lilyan, I'll tell you a secret—I'd love to do it again." And so we began to think about how she might be able to do *it* again, or other speeches. All of this opened a whole new world for Peggy.

It opened one for me as well, because something remarkable happens when I work with students, whether it's individually or in groups. Each one is unique; each one teaches me something; each one reaches a level of conviction that is different from any other— some more, some less, but that is what we strive for; that is our goal;

and that is what is at the core of conquering, overcoming, control-ling the fear of public speaking.

When Peggy Lynch revealed the pain of her personal remem-brances of shyness, inadequacy, and discomfort in class as a child, she was opening up a childhood traumatic experience. That, plus working at overcoming her fears of speaking before a group, was her way of finding her conviction. She didn't go through the emotional memory exercise as students in Lee Strasberg's class did, but after sharing her traumatic past with me she realized that she exorcises her demons through teaching, through encouraging her students' colorful language and their detailed drawings, and so on. Peggy identified with the special children she taught. Their trauma was similar to what she experienced as a child. She painstakingly, lov-ingly, and intelligently used her senses to bring out her students' sen-sory lives. Peggy was accepted by her audience of teachers because she revealed her personal love and strength of conviction, her belief in her students' capabilities. And it was that love and strength of conviction that enabled Peggy to speak to a large audience. Peggy's success speaking in front of 500 teachers was all the more dramatic when we remember the problems she had talking as a child.

Peggy Lynch had me as her practice audience, responding to her, nurturing and encouraging her. It is important to have one person or several people react to what you are saying. In being your own coach or teacher, you need to seek out such a person or audience. It's not easy, I know. But it's worth that time and energy, for the experience of speaking with conviction will define your speaking life and your day-to-day life. It happened for me; it happens for my students every day in private consultation, at the New School class, and with actual audiences. Knowing what propels you and using that knowl-edge by choosing words and pictures that stir you will in turn stir your audience.

You may not want or need to make a large-scale difference in your life or the lives of others. But whatever it is that you give is impor-tant. In order to give it, you must have conviction. In order to have conviction, you must connect to and believe in yourself. That is the process I hope you will continue to explore as you tackle the tech-niques of becoming a successful communicator. It takes commit-ment, practice, and discipline.

Assignment Seven

Give a talk of 15 minutes or more to a group of approximately 15 or more people on a subject you care passionately about. This speech is the culmination of the program. It will require the most work and can be the most rewarding.

1. Choose a subject of deep importance to you.

2. Plan to get a response, and structure your talk in the way that is second nature to you by now—middle first, then the end, then the beginning.

3. Prepare to connect to your own store of personal experience by doing a Private Moment exercise.

4. Now access that personal experience more deeply by doing an Affective Memory exercise.

5. Review the structure you planned and the points of your presentation, and remember the experiences of the Private Moment and Affective Memory exercises you have done.

6. Practice with a tape recorder. Critique yourself.

7. As you practice your talk, access the sensory connections.

8. You're on! Go out and give the speech. Record it.

9. Listen to the tape, and answer the questions in the Self-Critique Questionnaire for Step Seven.

10. Do Voice Exercise #7, as well as Voice Exercises #1 through #6 (see Appendix A).

Self-Critique Questionnaire for Step Seven

▶ How did sharing my private world with an audience help bring me to a new level of awareness while speaking?

▶ What was the benefit of allowing myself to be vulnerable?

▶ What were the reactions to my speech of conviction? (Point out at least three.)

▶ What could I do differently (better) next time?

SCHEDULE FOR WORKSHOP #7

This week, you will need to do Voice Exercises #1 to #7 on your own, before you meet.)

1. Prepare the room for the new audience.

2. Go around the room and have each person give his or her prepared speech to the entire audience, in the order determined at the last meeting.

3. After everyone has given their speeches, you should answer the Self-Critique Questionnaire for Step Seven and discuss your responses with your group. You may include the guests in the audience if it seems appropriate. If not, then try to meet as a group for a few minutes (away from the guests) in order to discuss your speeches.

The Seven Steps
in Action

*Now this is not the end. It is not
even the beginning of the end.
But it is, perhaps, the end
of the beginning.*

WINSTON CHURCHILL

You've come a long way since you first picked up this book. If you've done the work, you've equipped yourself with the skills and the insight to change, forever, the way you approach any speaking situation.

You know how to practice and experience your voice, how to get a response, structure your presentation, establish a dialogue, be creative, persuade, and have an objective. You know why you are speaking, to whom you are speaking, and what you want your listeners to take away with them. You are prepared to communicate from the depth of your convictions.

Three Compelling Examples of Fearless Speaking

The time has come to put all Seven Steps into action—every time you speak in public. They are a framework, a set of guiding principles, a safe harbor. Apply them, and speak fearlessly—as the students did in the examples that follow.

JEROME'S STORY
Welcome to the Brave New World of the Internet

Jerome is a sales executive for New Media, a division of the venerable news organization Reuters.

The New Media division, he explained on the first day of class, was formed to find ways to deliver news and advertising—the traditional staples of newspapers and magazines—to readers via the Internet.

Young, personable, and committed, Jerome is the ideal spokesman for the brave new world of online journalism and cybercommerce. A major part of his job is giving informational presentations to company employees and prospective users of the company's online service. But, he felt, his fear of public speaking diminished his effectiveness.

When Jerome talked about his job in conversation, he was lucid, animated, and entertaining. But when he got up to speak formally, his voice was thin and he sounded almost apologetic. His material was terrific, but his delivery seemed tentative and lacking in conviction.

He needed the Seven Step Program. And when he had completed it, the offstage and the onstage Jerome had become one and the same.

Here's a typical presentation of Jerome's, aided by PowerPoint, the computerized visual projection system that rapidly is becoming standard equipment for business presentations (more on its use later).

Jerome's topic: "The Internet and How Reuters Participates in It."

His audience: Any business or consumer group interested in the Internet as a business.

His objective: Inform his listeners about the rapid growth and immense reach of the Internet. Share with them his conviction that the Internet is the mainstream communication force of the future—and that Reuters is in the vanguard of this evolution.

His creative visual aid: PowerPoint-projected text consisting of bulleted points in his presentation.

BEGINNING

These are the words Jerome spoke (based on his outline), which he recorded and then transcribed.

Response-getter:

How many of you here tonight have signed on to the Internet in the last week? [Many hands go up.] Well, you had plenty of company—there are more than 70 million people online in North America alone.

Second response-getter, sets up dialogue:

How many of you have ever made a purchase over the Internet? [A few more hands.] You're not alone there, either—20 million of the 70 million have made purchases online.

Jerome tells them what he's going to tell them—that the tremendous growth of the Internet in the past few years is one of the greatest business stories of our time and that it's affected all of us. "I'd like to show you how, by showing you what the Internet now means to Reuters."

MIDDLE

Background:

I'm proud to tell you that Reuters' name is one of the great ones in the history of international journalism. It was founded more than 150 years ago, and now is a media giant.

Four years ago, this very old company launched into something very new: It formed its New Media division to find new markets for its content, and it invested in technology and other content companies. The goal of this division was to not only drive new revenue, but also to build a brand name known far better outside the U.S. media markets.

When New Media was formed:

- America Online was just starting.
- The Internet was not a public attraction.
- There was no Netscape . . . no Microsoft Explorer . . . Bill Gates didn't think the Internet would take off.

Tom, you were there. Seems like ancient history, doesn't it?
Now, Sally, we know what's happened since, don't we? Today:

- AOL is king of the online world . . . 13 million users and growing.
- Internet is mainstream.
- Netscape and Yahoo have market caps of over $6 billion.

So here we are, 70 million strong, online, and growing by 71,000 per day. 40 million of the 70 are in that golden demographic category—16 to 34. We who are online are fully 35 percent of all the adults in the United States!

It took radio 38 years to reach its first 50 million users. Television took 13. The Internet has done it in less than 5.

So, if you are among those who still think of the Internet as exotic and still largely in the future, I urge you think again.

What has all this meant for Reuters New Media?

It means—and this is, to me, an astounding and very gratifying development, so I want to emphasize it—it means we have made more money in the last two years from online publishers than from newspapers and magazines *combined*.

Why has this happened for Reuters?

- Advertisers want to be online, and are spending more than $1 billion a year to be there.
- The demographics are very strong, including growing usage by women, who make 80 percent of the purchasing decisions.
- People are spending more time online and less time watching television.
- At the same time, people have an appetite for content—news, sports, entertainment and health features, personal finance—like never before. (Example: 25 million people downloaded or viewed the Ken Starr report the first weekend it was available on the Internet.
- 53 percent of Internet users look at news on the Web daily.

END

New Media has accomplished the mission set by Reuters corporate headquarters: We've generated millions in new profits, and placed Reuters squarely where it wants to be—and, where I want to be—on the new frontier of global communication.

And the boom really has just begun.

Jerome did everything right in his presentation: He got a response and established a dialogue, structured his talk logically and persuasively, and used both creative language and visual aids as he spoke from a base of his own convictions about technology and the future.

And, in his presentation on the new world of communication and commerce made possible by computers, he *used* a computer—and used it wisely.

Instead of a traditional slide show to illustrate his points, Jerome used PowerPoint. For those who've never seen it in action, it's a software program that allows you to connect your laptop to a projector and display whatever is on your computer screen onto a larger screen or on the wall for an audience to share. The principal advantage is that a visual presentation can be created much more quickly, using all the myriad options that are available through the miracle of the computer.

The mistake untrained speakers often make is to assume the computer itself will do the work of the presentation. They invest countless hours into fussing over color tints and type fonts, then merely read to the audience what is projected on the screen.

Jerome didn't do that. He put *himself* into the presentation, using the text on the screen to underscore the dramatic, personalized, heartfelt points he was making.

No amount of high-tech wizardry will ever replace the power of one person communicating with another from a core of deeply held personal conviction. The tools may change, but the basics never will.

ELIZABETH'S STORY
How to Save Downtown

Elizabeth owns and operates a clothing store on the main street of a small Connecticut town. She grew up in the town and loves it dearly, thriving on its sense of community. And the heart of that community, she felt, was embodied in that homey little central business district where she ran her shop.

In her first session with me, she told me she was worried about the future of her downtown—and countless other downtowns all over the country. These business districts, she said, are threatened by malls and chain stores operated not by friends and neighbors, but by huge corporations.

She wanted to speak up on the subject, but her lifelong fear of speaking held her back. As the culmination of her work in the Seven Step Program, however, she went before her fellow Rotarians and gave the following talk.

Elizabeth's topic: "Living the Service Ideal of Rotary."

Her audience: Fellow members of her Rotary Club, all business and professional men and women who live and work in her Connecticut hometown.

Her objective: To persuade her fellow Rotarians that their downtown is worth saving and that it can be saved by applying Rotary ideals. And to suggest a specific plan for revitalizing downtown.

Her creative tools: Success stories dramatizing the small-town values of community and personal service.

BEGINNING

Every Main Street in America is struggling to survive, and ours is no exception. As you all know, we've lost our print shop, our jeweler, and our baker. We're all feeling discouraged and disillusioned.

Bob, how's your business since the new mall opened? . . . Jane, yours? . . . Well, mine, too.

Do you think we—business owners, managers, professionals—can survive in a sea of huge corporations, megafirms and shopping centers? [Mixed verbal response from audience: "Don't know . . . hope so . . . it's tough . . ."]

Summary:

Well, I believe we can survive, and prosper, too. And tonight, I want to tell you why and what we can do to take action.

MIDDLE

How do we compete with the big chain stores and corporations with bottomless pockets? [From audience: ". . . wish I knew . . ." people nod, shake their heads.]

Here's my view: The way to compete is to follow your dreams and live in the service of Rotary ideals. We can apply the Four-Way Test. If you do this, you will ride the wave, turn the tide, and achieve competitive advantage.

The words of the Four-Way Test are as true today as ever: Of the things we think, say, or do:

1. Is it the truth?
2. Is it fair to all concerned?
3. Will it build goodwill and better friendships?
4. Will it be beneficial to all concerned? [Murmurs of agreement.]

Some would find such thinking hopelessly idealistic. But here are two stories that illustrate practical ways to live the service ideal.

Story number 1: Tom made and sold Tom's of Maine toothpaste, made of natural products, because he believed such products served people better. Based on that ideal, he built a company of smart young people and marketed his idea as well as his product. How many of you brush your teeth with Tom's of Maine? Come on, don't be shy. Hmm.

Four out of twenty-five. Not bad. The lesson is this: By being true to himself and his values, he was true to his customers and he succeeded.

How can you be truer to yourselves and your customers and revitalize downtown? What were your dreams and values when you started in your business? Have they gotten buried? Do they need to be revived? [A few answer, nod in agreement.] Here's another true story.

Story number 2: In a nearby town, Main Street business owners reacted when business was down by isolating themselves from each other and retreating into their stores. One creative restaurant owner decided to be proactive: He invited his fellow business owners to an open house at which everyone got to air their feelings. From this meeting grew a merchants' association that sponsored such successful community activities as a jazz festival, a cook-off, and a big community Christmas party. The efforts paid off in more traffic and more business.

Applying these Rotary ideals of service to community can save our town.

Remember what fun we had staging our 75th and 100th anniversary celebrations? And how successful they were? Well, why can't we do that on an ongoing basis?

I propose that the Rotary start a merchants' group that will plan a series of events to rebuild downtown. A classic auto show and an art fair would be good places to start. But first, let's have a dinner at Mack's restaurant and talk about ways to get our lost businesses back.

END

The stories of Tom's of Maine and the successful merchants' group in our neighboring town are living examples of our ideals of service. One, they represent fundamental truths; two, they treat people fairly; three, they build good and lasting relationships; and four, they are beneficial to all our citizens.

When we apply our Rotarian ideals to business we will get results—and compete with the giant shopping centers.

I challenge you to believe and act as if Rotary can make a difference in renewing hope in our community by revitalizing our downtown.

Elizabeth's fearless speech was a success. Following the Seven Step Program, she learned how to practice and rework the text of the speech, she was able to get over her fear of speaking. The dinner she called for was held. So were the auto show and the art fair. When last heard from, Elizabeth's Main Street was fighting back—

and she was so pleased with her speaking experience that she made plans to take her talk to other Rotary Clubs.

JULIA'S STORY
Welcome Back, Class of '48

Julia is a retired United Nations administrator. Despite her lifelong fear of speaking, she enjoyed her career, traveling throughout the world and doing work she believed in deeply.

Her fear of speaking is rooted in a childhood trauma. When she was 14, her mother abandoned her and her older sister. Julia says she always believed that she was a burden to her depressed mother and that she should be silent and self-effacing in order to relieve some of that burden. However, Julia spoke up only when she felt strongly about something. Thus, in her child's eyes, her mother's departure was evidence that speaking up at all was the wrong thing to do. Julia told me:

> She went to Canada for her father's funeral. That was in early December, and she said she would be back for Christmas, but she wasn't. She said her stepmother needed her, and she'd be back in early January.
>
> And then it began, for my sister and myself, the agonizing and increasingly less hopeful wait as one deadline after another passed, until our (alcoholic) father gave her an ultimatum to return. And at last, the fearful hoping was over. Our mother wasn't coming back. We really must have been too much of a burden for her. She hadn't even said good-bye. She never explained. She had been with us constantly for all of my 14 years, and then she had simply left.
>
> Now I was terrified. I had continued to speak up in the face of evidence that to do so was unwise and the ultimate had happened. I had driven my mother away.
>
> Since then my life has been darkened by this pervasive sorrow. My career in international relations certainly was diminished by my fear of speaking in groups. I never asked a question at a meeting. I never made a comment. I never seconded a motion. The problem is evidenced socially as well. Given the fact that six or eight people represent "the public" to me, and evoke my fear of public speaking, does not make me a sought-after dinner party guest.

However, Julia never stopped struggling to overcome her fear. Several medications that weren't available when she was younger now help relieve her anxiety. And she has worked hard to overcome her fear of speaking.

When Julia entered my class, she was barely audible. She never initiated a conversation or asked a question. She just waited until someone asked her a question. Then when she answered, she spoke in sentence fragments. Her breathing was constricted, and her voice was shaky. We worked hard on diaphragmatic breathing and vocalization. Through the Seven Step Program, Julia made enormous progress. She practiced her voice exercises diligently. She allowed herself to be vulnerable by telling the events that led to her mother's departure. She was open in class about the hurt she felt. And she sought therapeutic counseling, as well as pharmacological expertise.

Now Julia seeks out opportunities to speak. Here's a talk she gave to a group of young college-bound women.

> *Julia's topic:* "The 50th Reunion of the Brown University Class of 1948."
>
> *Her audience:* Young college-bound women, their parents, and their teachers.
>
> *Her objective:* Persuade her listeners of the value of a Brown education; give them some historical perspective on the great social changes that have occurred since 1948; emphasize all this with memories of her own Brown experience and what it means to her today.

BEGINNING

> Not long ago, I walked in the annual Brown graduation procession with about 150 other returning alumna from my class—some 70 of whom were women—all about my age (which I leave you to figure out) and all members of the class of 1948.
>
> As we passed by the Class of 1998—all of them only a few years older than you—the young graduates gave us an ovation I'll never forget.
>
> *Response-getter:*
>
> Do you realize that your grandmother could have been in that group? [The students laugh and applaud.]

Tell them what you're going to tell them:

At that moment, I felt a solidarity between two distant generations that made me proud of the university we all attended. Men and women live together in a very different world today. In 1948, women had obstacles placed before them that may seem unimaginable to you. But the struggle was worth it. And that's what I want to talk to you about today.

MIDDLE

This year I attended the 50th reunion of my graduating class. Back in '48 we were known as Pembrokers, Pembroke College being the women's college of Brown University.

That was so long ago—do you know who was president then? [Students: "Wow . . . Kennedy? . . . Nixon? . . ."] No, it was Harry Truman.

The women still walked behind the men in the graduation procession. And there were places on campus where women weren't allowed without a man. Women students were discouraged from majoring in some of the more scientific fields—and sometimes, informally, from even taking such courses. There were separate classes for men and women, where feasible. Seems incredible now, doesn't it? But we worked with and around these barriers as best we could.

Brown University was founded in 1764, but didn't admit women until 1891—127 years later. The women's college of Brown University became Pembroke in 1927 and survived as a separate college until 1971.

When we entered Pembroke in 1944, World War II was still in full force, and there weren't many men in sight. The war had changed the atmosphere in just about every respect. Gone were the days of swallowing goldfish and climbing up greased flagpoles. We were more serious, I think. We had fun, but we also rolled bandages for the Red Cross and did airplane spotting and the like. And in 1945, when the war ended, we danced in the streets of downtown Providence.

Not long after V-J Day, the day Japan surrendered, the men started coming back to Brown. These were men made mature by war and, in many cases, men with families, living in Quonset huts hastily thrown up on a playground next to Brown Stadium.

And there we were, with Rosie the Riveter as role model—women who had "manned" the home front and defense industry, quite literally—being thrust back into all-male and all-female classes whenever possible and frequently with the men's class getting the full professor and the women's getting a graduate student.

I had no intention of being relegated to what were traditionally the courses women took, so I majored in a new interdepartmental offering, International Relations—which, eventually, led me to a long, interesting, and, when overseas, a fascinating and exciting career at the United Nations.

Here's one incident that I think is especially illustrative of a certain mind-set of the time. The political science department offered a prize (money) for the best essay on a designated subject—number of words: 5,000—and I wrote a paper. However, mine was a lot less than 5,000 words, but I felt I had made my point.

The professor certainly did not agree. He announced in class that one of the members seemed to think that political scientists couldn't do mathematics. He went on and on, finally saying that he didn't like having girls in his classes because they did well on exams, thereby raising the curve, but they didn't contribute anything to the class!

There were four women, including me, in that particular class, and we said nothing. Can you picture that in today's classroom?

As I said before, there were places on campus where women were not welcome, one of which was called the Blue Room. It was—we thought then—an elegant lounge where one could get such things as ice cream sodas—but only if accompanied by a man. We complained about that, so the university opened a women-only soda fountain on the Pembroke side.

Big deal! [Gets a laugh.]

Anyhow, the Blue Room still exists. Today it is neither elegant nor blue. And women and men mix there freely.

END

And now it's the year of the 50th reunion. We marched in the commencement procession, and the class of '98 applauded us, and it turned out to be one of those really memorable experiences.

I always wondered what was so great about a 50th reunion, other than the big fuss made about it, but now I think I know. The big fuss is good. It provides a special chance to relive old times with old classmates. It provides a time to give yourself a pat on the back for whatever you appreciate from the past 50 years. And it provides time, and circumstances, for a lot of reflection.

Julia doesn't know if her eloquent soft sell has recruited any future Brown alumna. But she does know that her voice is now an instrument she can use more freely and strongly. She can initiate discussions and she can stand in front of a group of people without trembling. Most important, she knows she has something of value to share with her listeners. And that she can share her story with an increasing sense of enjoyment that was a long time coming.

EXERCISE: PRACTICE OUTLINING SPEECHES

Here's a fun test for you:

Choose one, two, or all three of the speeches presented in this chapter to break down into outlines. What we have here, as we have in all the steps from Two to Seven of the Fearless Speaking Program are three compelling and very well organized speeches. I think it would be to your advantage to figure out the objective of each speech and then put each of them into outline form. You could also track the Seven Steps to see how and if the speakers used them.

Beginning (intro)—Tell them what you're going to tell them.
    I.
    II.

Middle (body)—Tell them.
    I.
        A.
           1.
           2.
        B.
        C.
    II.

End (conclusion)—Tell them what you told them.
    I.
    II.

This should help solidify for you:

1. How to construct an outline
2. Language you could use based on the outline
3. The value of speaking from an outline
4. The use of the Seven Steps in every speech you give

This would be a good time to take another test. Several weeks ago (see page 32 in Step One), you took a vocal inventory of your sound. Go back to that test and take it again. Then turn to the page in your large notebook where you wrote down your original response. Compare it with the response to your voice critique today.

Special Situations

*How many cares one loses when
one decides not to be something
but to be someone.*

Coco Chanel

Here are examples of how the Seven Steps are used in special situations that most of us need to experience at some time in our lives:

- Meetings, panel discussions, recruitment
- Introductions, toasts, roasts, and awards
- Conference calls
- Job and media interviews
- Eulogies

The Seven Steps, intelligently and creatively applied, won't let you down. Organized as an outline, they form an excellent foundation for any planned communication—even those that happen on the spur of the moment.

Meetings, Panel Discussions, Recruitment

The following examples illustrate special situations that involve planning to brainstorm, discuss, and recruit.

Meetings

Though many meetings have the semblance of spontaneous discussion, in reality, they demand planning and preparation on the part of the speakers. Here's how Brian used the steps to take control of ineffective meetings.

Brian is a computer engineer, the recently promoted creative vice president of a small high-tech firm that specializes in computer designs for giant electronic billboards, like the ones in Times Square in New York City. With the CEO on the road often, Brian was left to oversee ongoing projects and preside at weekly update meetings on them. Suddenly he had two problems: his fear of speaking and a lack of focus during the weekly meetings.

He told me, "I don't know how to control these people, and they know it. I begin by asking so-and-so what the progress is on project B, and all hell breaks loose. Two people start arguing about some detail. . . . The teams become combative. . . . I'm just the sweating, shaking pawn at the end of the table . . . instead of being a project manager, I've deteriorated into a sort of on-the-scene reporter, taking notes on chaos . . ."

Most people know that in order to have a successful meeting, the group needs to have a common goal. But too often that goal is formulaic.

Brian's problem was that he was just following the formula—asking for project updates and costs—instead of setting his own long-term objective. I told him to determine what it was and write that down.

He wrote: "I want to play a central role in assisting and overseeing the company's ongoing projects, thereby lowering the company's costs, and proving my value to the CEO."

To assert his authority at the next meeting, Brian wrote an outline of points he wanted to make. Then he took charge of the meeting from the start:

> These are the current numbers on the setup costs for the XYZ project—orders total $5,674.80, of which $428.60 are duplicates of orders we made a week ago for the same project. In three weeks I've found duplicate orders totaling $6,866.40. That means, simply, we bought stuff you guys—Mike, Sherie, Jim, and Elaine—could have gotten from you guys—Ed, Tim, and Doug—free! With the boss's approval, I've decided to stop this last order. How do you want to coordinate sharing this stuff so we can keep the costs down?

With that opening, he got an immediate response. Everyone gasped. Then there was silence. Then someone made a suggestion, and the dialogue began.

"It got raucous once, and I could feel myself getting tense," he said, "but I managed to interrupt and say, 'Get back to Point C,' or whatever it was on my outline, and they did."

Brian kept his remarks in order and made sure he started out with something that got the response he needed. But the key to working through his fear was determining his own objective, then structuring the meeting to actively pursue it.

Having established his authority in that meeting, he went on to assert his own creative ideas and help find solutions to design problems. His acknowledged objective, to build a niche for himself in the company, became an organizing tool, helping him act rather than react—and, in the process, speak fearlessly.

Panel Discussions

Ellie, a contract attorney who recently joined a major film company, was mortified by her failure to speak up at a prestigious panel discussion at a national convention. Despite her careful preparation, she said, she was intimidated and finally overpowered by bolder speakers on the panel.

". . . [O]ne of the big guns started off, just took over, and the other big gun took over from him. And suddenly I felt like a little girl at the dinner table listening to the adults. I didn't know how to enter into the discussion. At one point they deferred to me, but by then my throat had closed off. And when I began to talk I skipped the thing I'd planned to say first. . . . I was like the incredible shrinking woman."

Ellie had prepared the content of her remarks. But she hadn't thought about how to get into the discussion in order to give those remarks. She had not planned an opening statement that would get a response and thereby provide her the focal point from which to speak.

When she realized she would have to fight for time and space, like one of the guests on CNN's *Crossfire*, she also realized she had no tools to do so—no anecdotes, analogies, quotes, humorous asides—

nothing to insert into the ongoing conversation. She had not planned in a creative way. She had planned only the basic content of her remarks and nothing more.

Furthermore, she needed a strong voice to build her confidence, and she didn't have that, either.

She needed a voice, a tactical plan for getting response, and creative attention-grabbers to regain focus and make her points.

Ellie volunteered to be on another convention panel to get more practice. This time she began by getting a response:

> I'd like to see a show of hands. How many think they know what an entertainment lawyer does? . . . Now how many know what a contract lawyer does? . . . Well, I'm here to tell you they are one and the same, except one sounds sexier."

With such a strong opening, she got everyone's attention. And because the panel included two other contract lawyers and two entertainment lawyers, she assured herself a lively role in the discussion, which dealt with changing media technology and in contract law.

She came armed with entertaining examples taken from film and television, like this anecdote about American film representatives negotiating with Asian importers regarding safeguards against video piracy:

> We didn't want to lose millions to video pirates the minute we put our movies in the stores. We decided to be very exact with our language describing just how they can import our videos and to whom they can sell them. We put every detail into our contract to make it airtight. We thought we were brilliant until we saw the contracts printed up in several Asian languages—Japanese, Cantonese, Korean. One little slash of ink changes a whole sentence. Our language experts said: "Don't do this! You cannot police all of Asia in all the different Asian languages." Whereupon she held up one page of a contract in English, and two corresponding pages of its translation into Korean. "You want a simple idea, in simple language, that translates!" We ended up putting a price on the videos that would cover a certain amount of our losses, and we cut out half of what we'd written.

Because she began to develop a stronger, healthier, more assertive voice . . . because she came prepared with visual illustrations and anecdotes to keep her audience's attention . . . Ellie did not experience the panic she felt the first time she served on a panel.

She told me, "That's the first time I can remember volunteering comments, instead of sitting there dreading my turn to speak. I was nervous, but I felt 'excited' nervous, not 'sick' nervous."

Recruitment

Marsha, a junior college administrator, was asked to meet with small groups of parents of local high schoolers. The purpose was student recruitment, convincing these parents, most of whom didn't go to college, that her school was right for their children. But, despite organizing what she thought was a strong case for attending her college, she felt that she failed.

Her problem was that she recited her 15-minute pitch, rarely looking up, never speaking to her listeners. As a result, she received few questions and no real expression of interest.

Marsha's mission was to use the meetings as forums for discussion. But because of her fear of speaking, she behaved as if she wanted to avoid discussion—to avoid dialogue—at every turn.

Marsha reorganized her presentation. She had a great story to tell, which began by getting a response, and led to dialogue.

> Hi. My name is Marsha. My great-grandfather died in a coal mine accident when he was 32. My grandfather worked in the same coal mine. He died when he was 49. My Dad got out of the coal mines when he was 28 and became a trucker. My brother got out with this (she held up a junior college diploma). And I followed my brother. Who here knows what the occupation of his great-grandfather was?

She interviewed each person in the group and guided the discussion with such questions as "What do you think are the major reasons people don't go to college?" and "What would you need to send your child to college?"

She answered the questions with anecdotes and illustrations that explained how her college could meet the financial and practical needs of the high schoolers. She concluded by giving everyone a packet of brochures detailing courses, the variety of times classes are offered, and payment plans. Then she set out a pad and pencil and asked everyone to leave a phone number for a follow-up call.

She said later, "I felt tense at the beginning, but I thought if I want them to open up to me, I should open up to them. And my own family background is a pretty good argument for education. This time I think it worked. People got the message. It felt good."

Brian, Ellie, and Marsha learned valuable lessons. These include:

- Don't assume that, because you and your listeners or fellow panel members are all sitting in a circle facing one another or around a conference table, that you have rapport. When you plan and get an initial response, you establish a positive relationship with your listeners.

- Don't assume that, because you're not in charge of the meeting, you shouldn't have a goal. Give careful thought to why you are there. If you don't consider your underlying goal, you're apt to dissipate your energies fighting nervousness that arises from not really knowing what you're doing there rather than contributing to the process by offering your input. This is a key point that applies to any speaking situation.

- Structure your remarks in a way that invites an affirmation of your view. If you are working toward building a consensus, the focus of the interchange will be the topic, not you. Everyone will feel productive, and your fears will dissolve in the group interchange.

Introductions, Toasts, Roasts, Awards

Short, personal speeches like introductions, toasts, roasts, and acceptance of awards place their own special kind of pressure on the speaker.

On occasions like these, it's easy to feel that a witty performance is required—and that if wit is not delivered, the speech is not successful.

It's hard not to feel this way, as short, entertaining speeches like these are widely regarded as a specialized art form. Speech anthologies often have a special section devoted to them—collections of examples of clever remarks by Mark Twain, John F. Kennedy, Oliver Wendell Holmes, Adlai Stevenson.

Adding to that expectation are the roasts we see on television, in which comedians and other celebrities, armed with professionally written jokes, kid each other mercilessly and hilariously.

So, the minute someone asks us to introduce the keynote speaker, or toast the retiring vice president, or roast the groom, or present the company's annual award for excellence, the fear appears like a dark cloud. How can I possibly measure up, you wonder?

You can—here's how.

Opening Remarks/Introduction

Claudia, a Wall Street financial advisor, was asked to make the opening remarks for her firm's annual charity auction and introduce the auctioneer. It was a social occasion with a large business burden attached.

"It's a social situation . . . But it's work, too," she explained to the class, "because everyone is watching you socialize either successfully or ineptly. And when it comes time to hand out the big accounts, the ones that require 'people' skills, judgments are going to be made based in part on what they thought of you at the auction. I'm always anxious about speaking, but this is really tough."

Claudia wrote an introduction and read it to the class:

> Ladies and Gentlemen, thank you all for being here. This year it is my pleasure to introduce Bill Strouthers as our auctioneer. He has overseen the arrangement of the beautiful objects you have been viewing during the evening, and he is eager to field your bids. Remember that your bids will be supporting Mercy Hospital's purchase of another kidney dialysis machine, and be generous. Thank you.

She told us she felt "awful" and that her hands shook while giving her "boring" speech. "I don't want to try to be witty," she said. "I just want to say what I have to say."

And what did she really want to say? That was her problem: She didn't know.

She wanted to say how highly she regarded Bill, a friend who had asked that she introduce him—and she wanted to shine in front of prospective clients.

"I feel like I'm supposed to be a circus ringmaster, but they picked the wrong person," she said.

"Why not be a ringmaster?" someone suggested. "Get the musicians to give you a drum roll and everything."

In jest, Claudia showed up the next week with a pair of cymbals and gave her introduction this way:

> Ladies and gentlemen! [Clash!] Our auction for the one and only Mercy Hospital is about to begin! [Clash!] Our inestimable volunteers, led by Joe Santini, have combed the globe to assemble an array of artifacts, gadgets, and glamour worthy only of royalty, and you. And now may I present the one person capable of handling the auspicious responsibility of auctioneer—our own investment partner Bill Strouthers! [Clash!] Bill is graced with an abundance of wit, a sense of fair play, and the clear, unwavering certainty that market competition defines value. And now, compete with gusto! Remember every dollar will help buy a kidney patient another chance. May the bidding begin! [Clash, Clash!]

The class loved Claudia's remarks, and her hands stopped shaking when she used the cymbals. She asked the drummer in the dance band to add a drum roll. People loved the circus feeling. Because she tapped her own sense of humor and her own repartee, it worked.

Toasts

Charles, a financial analyst, dreaded what appeared to be a plum assignment: giving a toast at a dinner honoring a well-known financial wizard, a man of legendary status.

"No one at my company knows how difficult this is for me," he complained. "My peers think this is an honor. They don't know I'd rather anyone else do it but me."

Practicing on the class, Charles wrote and delivered a stiff, formal toast in which he attempted to get a response with a literary reference that sounded highbrow but was really hard to follow.

"Tell us how you *really* feel about this man," I said. And Charles did, in a stream of praise that could have lasted an hour.

I told him to take the tape recording of what he had just said, listen to it, and extract material for his toast. He did and came up with a heartfelt, straightforward toast.

Charles began with a question:

Who knows what $1,000 invested with our guest of honor at the beginning of his career in 1956 would be worth today? [Joan took a guess.] Joan, you're close, but still way off. The answer is $8 million.

Charles went on to summarize his hero's stunning success and illustrate it with a playful metaphor. The modest guest of honor had claimed no credit for making his clients rich in 1995—a year, he said, when "any fool could make money in the stock market. To paraphrase President Kennedy, 'A rising tide lifts all yachts.'"

> Mr. Buffett, in a sea of winning investment ideas, you are the cruise ship. We are mere seagulls hovering overhead for scraps of information.

When Charles thought about why his toast was such a success, he realized he had stopped worrying about being erudite or witty, and put his attention to reflecting his beliefs. As is so often the case, his own words proved to be quite eloquent. He said he felt emotional giving the toast, "but emotional in a good way. I felt connected to everybody in the room."

Roasts

Margaret, a mild-mannered attorney and private person, was asked to roast the guest of honor at her law association's annual benefit.

But the idea of coming up with mock insults for fun didn't appeal to her. Worse, she was accustomed to reading carefully prepared texts, never speaking from an outline.

She decided that, rather than go for the insults, she would *persuade* her listeners, tongue in cheek, that the guest of honor, a female partner in a large firm, can teach young lawyers the most important career survival skills. Margaret deadpanned:

> We all know Marilou is a successful partner in one of our larger firms. What you don't know is the wealth of knowledge she brings to the art of surviving a legal career. I am here tonight to launch the Marilou Salon, a finishing school for all those hoping to succeed, as Marilou has, in a world of coffee, copiers, and recycled air. A sampling of her wisdom . . .

Then, as if she were making a case to a jury, she listed Marilou's office habits and dictums, which everyone present would recognize.

Women, wear tights, not hose. No matter how much the firm pays you it's not enough to keep you in hose without runs.

Use a great deal of hand cream, everybody . . .

Disguise rapid aging by mentioning, at every opportunity, how wonderful it was to go sky diving this year . . .

This wisdom, and more, is available to you at the Marilou Salon.

Marilou has a free introductory offer. Anyone who can carry 30 or more pounds of legal briefs at one time will be given one month's free instruction. Don't delay. She's a very special lady.

"I wasn't as nervous," she said later, "because I structured the thing like a sales pitch, and that's sort of what I'm doing most of the time, convincing people to take this or that action. I had a direction that felt familiar. Also, I knew that everything I said pertained to Marilou, so every line got a laugh. That made it easier to get through the roast. That's what I was hoping for."

The key here is Margaret's statement: "I knew that everything I said pertained to Marilou, so every line got a laugh." Make sure your audience is in on everything you say, and, like comedians, arm yourself with insurance. Have a few extra comments in your pocket to support the really big laughs or to detract from a weak spot.

Awards

Jane, an architect, was asked to give the annual company award to Bob, her boss, who also was her mentor and friend. She knew he hated awards and sentimental speeches. Worse, she had a fear of speaking. The chore looked impossible to her.

I told her to write two speeches—the one she thought she was expected to give and one that said what she really thought about Bob.

Then we put the two together in a blend of irreverence and affection, with the following result. She got an immediate and continual response.

Bob Smith has been a wonderful mentor and friend to me. He taught me what an architect is. We have a glamorous job [laughter]. Make lots of money [laughter]. Have fun drawing and doodling all day [laughter]. It's a gentleman's profession. You just sit in your oak-paneled office and arrange your Tinkertoys [laughter and applause].

He is indeed a gentleman. Bob is what we all should be, a very good listener, the best space saver New York City ever had [applause], an educator [applause], and whenever he can be, a renegade [cheers].

When I arrived here, I figured out pretty quickly that it's not like it was in school. As yet no one has expressed an interest in funding my own particular blueprint for a new city. But Bob has been doing this for 20 years and what he's done seems worth it [applause]. On behalf of the firm, I want to thank you, Bob, for accepting this award. We know you wouldn't accept it unless you plan to be here another 20 years. Congratulations [applause].

To summarize: Once you find your key to a particular task, the steps follow.

- Claudia realized that introducing the auctioneer gave her a chance to show her "people skills," a very important ability to have in her business.
- Charles felt stiff and tense until he realized that he needed to speak from his particular awareness of who the guest of honor was.
- Margaret didn't feel comfortable doing a roast until she trusted her own unique sense of humor.
- Jane couldn't come up with anything to say until she thought about her bold, yet respectful, way of looking at Bob.

Conference Calls

Get a Response: In conducting a conference call, it's important to plan what you want to say to establish rapport, and get a response from the person or teleconferencing group you are talking to. If it's a group, acknowledge the presence of everyone: "Tom, in Des Moines? How are you? And Jill, at the home office? Good to talk to you . . ." Making this connection will prepare for the dialogue you want to initiate, just as you would in a face-to-face presentation.

Identify Your Objective: Jot down notes and organize your thoughts beforehand. Anticipate possible reactions to what you have to say. The process of reviewing your objective prior to calling will help you formulate key phrases and structure your statements to achieve your goal. With an outline in front of you, you will have focus, which will involve you, as well as the group.

Job and Media Interviews

Being interviewed for a job and being interviewed by a television, radio, or print reporter may seem very different at first glance. But they have much in common, and that's why I'm grouping them together.

The prospect of doing either kind of interview is certain to upset anyone who has fear of speaking.

What could be worse than sitting across a desk from an interrogator, whose job it is to give a thumbs-up or thumbs-down on your next career move? Or facing the unblinking eye of a television camera in the spotlight?

Know very clearly why you are participating in the interview and what you hope to achieve from it.

In the case of a job interview, the answer to that question may seem obvious: Your objective is to get the job.

But is it that simple? Are you clear on why you want this particular job? How it fits into your plan for the future? What you expect from it? What compromises or concessions, if any, you are willing to make to get it? Are you prepared to speak to every point raised?

Do you know why you want to work for this company? Do they really offer what you want? Is there information you need from your interviewer to help you make those decisions?

In the case of a media interview, determining your objective is no less essential.

Begin by asking yourself, why am I doing this?

Any reporter who is doing the job correctly will help you focus on your objective by introducing him- or herself and stating the purpose properly:

"My name is . . ."

"I'm a reporter (or producer) for . . ."

"I'm doing a story on . . ."

"I want to interview you because . . ."

The last of these four is the most important to you. What does this reporter specifically want to know from you? What does this reporter believe you have to add to the story?

A tip: *Beware of any reporter who is vague about what he or she is doing. If you aren't certain, ask some questions of your own before you consent to the interview. You are entitled to have clear answers to the preceding four questions.*

If you're doing the interview because your job requires it, know exactly what your company's message is and what you, as a professional in your job, have to say about it.

Remember: If you are there for your company, you are also there for yourself. You want to represent your company, its philosophy, its products, its position properly. But you want to serve your own higher objective, too.

Job Interview

Knowing why you are there and focusing on your message will help you put your energy where it belongs—into communication, not fear.

Having thought through and determined your objective, the next step is to *structure* what you plan to say. Obviously, you can't script either type of interview. But you can know your message, even have a few notes in front of you, and try to anticipate questions.

Structure your thoughts in what I call "mini-speeches."

A mini-speech is just what it suggests: a short, structured statement that has a beginning, a middle, and an end—fashioned to meet its objective. Consider the following example.

Frances was planning for an important job interview. One of the points she wanted to make to her prospective employer was that, although she had moved several times over the past four years to accommodate her husband's job, she intended to settle in the area and commit to long-term employment.

She knew she needed a good statement regarding her "flight risk." At an appropriate time in the interview, she volunteered:

My husband and I love this community. First of all we were able to buy twice the house for less money than what our house in California cost. Secondly, the schools here are excellent, and since we have a

10-year-old and a 12-year-old who need to put down roots in good schools, we feel we've hit the jackpot. We're here to stay.

The mini-speech enables you to take charge of an interview—or, at least, take charge of your own input and keep it flowing. Instead of feeling powerless and dependent on the interviewer for your success, you can organize your thoughts and come into the interview with a set of statements that keep you focused on your goals, rather than your fear.

There may be three, four, or more central points you want to make. Summarize them for yourself, first in a theme statement, then in specific points in an outline. From there, you can break your points into separate mini-speeches. Use them as you answer the questions put to you.

TV Interviews

The mini-speech helps you anticipate questions. And it helps you provide the kind of succinct, quotable answers that tend to get used, especially on television, where a good sound byte is prized.

Also, the mini-speech prepares you for interviewers who, themselves, aren't well prepared—rookie reporters, for instance, or untrained interviewers who are even more frightened than you are. By providing them with your mini-speeches—in effect, answers to questions they haven't asked but should have—you are doing them, as well as yourself, a service.

The mini-speech can also help you prevent the interview from straying away from your objective, if you use another technique I call "bridging."

Think of a bridge as just that—it transports you from one place to another. In speaking, it means taking charge of the direction of the discussion. You can answer the interviewer's question directly, and leave it at that. Or you can take the opportunity to make a separate point, by addressing the question and then making a transition, or bridging, to the point you want to make.

I'm not suggesting that you duck questions or try to take the reporter's story away from him or her. A good reporter won't let you do that, anyway. But you can get your own message across in the context of a broader story if you have prepared properly and look for opportunities to do so.

Bridging works best when your objective is related to, or can support, the reporter's objective. (If you know your objective is wildly different from the reporter's, you probably shouldn't be doing the interview in the first place.)

Here's an example. A reporter is doing a story on needy senior citizens going hungry in your community and is interviewing you because you are the volunteer coordinator of Citymeals-on-Wheels, a charitable organization that delivers meals to shut-ins. You want to communicate that Citymeals-on-Wheels delivered 1,638,757 hot meals to elderly shut-ins in 1998 and will top that number in 1999, that your organization is funded by charitable contributions, and that you are always looking for more volunteers especially at holiday time.

The question may be: "Sally, how bad is the hunger problem here? How many of our elderly aren't getting enough to eat?"

Your answer: "There are still too many, Tom. They're proud people, and reluctant to come forth and ask for help. But we're finding them. Last year, Citymeals-on-Wheels delivered 1,638,757 meals. This year there will be an increase of at least 1,000 men and women who are dependent on us for sustenance. One hundred percent of contributions from the general public are used exclusively for the preparation and delivery of meals."

When you know what you want to say and have outlined how you want to say it, practice breaking up your overall statement with a series of questions that you can answer in small, 30-second bytes. Practice out loud before the interview.

When the moment comes, you will be in control, setting forth points you want to make as opportunities arise—and creating your own opportunities to make points by bridging to the information you want to share. The result will be a conversation you planned and conducted to reach your objective.

Use lively metaphors and analogies to illustrate your points. A complex idea, which may normally require five minutes to explain, can be expressed in seconds if you find the right analogy. Following are some examples.

On September 2, 1998, Elizabeth Farnsworth, of the *Newshour with Jim Lehrer* on PBS, interviewed several experts on Russia on the subject of the Russian economic crisis and its threat to the global economy and political stability, and President Clinton's impending summit with Russian president Boris Yeltsin.

Professor Melor Sturua, a former Russian citizen, now professor at the University of Minnesota, cut through an abstract discussion of Clinton's diplomacy with the following analogy:

> Let me abandon some sophisticated vocabulary and give you an example. Somebody's dying from massive coronary heart attack. And the doctor tells him, "I will treat you, but you have to abandon smoking, drinking . . . you must jog, you must run, etc. That's fine. But the man is dying. You must treat him *now*. You must apply some intensive cardiovascular therapy. . . . All conditions [to economic aid] are iffy conditions. Health is very iffy. If it's too late, it doesn't matter . . . to the man, or to Russia.

Prof. Sturua's strong Russian accent enhanced his eloquence.

Later in the same interview, Prof. Sturua held up two credit cards to the camera:

> May I show you two credits? One is an ordinary MasterCard, another is Mostcard, issued by the Most Bank, which is the fifth largest bank in Russia. When you insert in money machine MasterCard, you get dollars. When you insert Mostcard, you get just a flash on the screen—"All the transactions temporarily suspended." So now based in Russia, we have temporarily suspended free market, and temporarily suspended democracy. I hope temporarily, but suspended.

Job and media interviews require you to *incorporate* the message you want to give into a discussion with another person. To do that, first you have to plan what it is you want to say, and why you want to say it. Then you can use your creativity to fashion your higher objective and successfully persuade your interviewer of your case.

- The *mini-speech* allows you to plan for interruptions and still make the points you want to make. Break up your message into small, short statements that you can share at the right opportunity.

- *Bridging* allows you to make your points, regardless of whether the interviewer sets a stage for you by asking the "right" questions. You can take charge of the discussion by addressing the question and then transitioning to the point you want to make.

- Use *creative analogies* that illuminate the subject and allow you to express your thoughts in fewer words. Remember that media interviews are usually very short, so the time is precious. Vivid images and short sentences are often most effective.

Eulogies

Eulogies are crafted from one's most private feelings, spoken in a very public setting. The speaker and audience both have heightened sensitivities. They gather together under highly charged emotional circumstances, hoping to find solace and sense in the words shared. I have never known anyone who gave a eulogy without fear and racking self-doubt.

Here's how telling a story helped me get through the first moments of a eulogy I was asked to give for Jessica Savitch, the television anchorwoman who died in a tragic car accident in 1984.

Long before it was my turn to speak at the memorial service, my heart began to beat loud and fast, and my throat became so restricted that no sound would come out. I had asked the minister to have a glass of water handy for me at the lectern. I kept humming the melodies of the psalms that were sung. I tried to sing the words, but no sound came.

When I climbed the high, marble steps to the pulpit I saw the water waiting for me. I looked out at the audience and was overwhelmed by the sight of all those sad, expectant eyes staring back.

Amid tears, I tried to see the words I'd written down. I had planned to begin the eulogy with an amusing story about Jessica, and I am grateful that it stayed with me in that moment. I opened my mouth and, perhaps because I was in the presence of God, sound did come out. I began to talk.

> Jessica came to me for voice work and general polishing of presentation techniques back in 1975. After every lesson, I was left with *more*. More information, more involvement, more appreciation of life, more fun. She had a way of turning things around—the most devastating or annoying—so that we both ended up laughing at it. Just last week on a plane to Minneapolis, the gentleman sitting next to me, who owns a television station in Duluth, said that he recalled Bill Monroe of *Meet the Press* chiding Jessica about being both beautiful

and an anchor. Bill was a nice-looking man, who happened to be bald. He said something to the effect of, "I guess you have to be both beautiful and smart to be an anchor, but what if you weren't beautiful, then what would you do?" Without missing a beat, Jessica responded, "I guess I'd have to be on *Meet the Press*."

With that story, I got a response from the audience. People didn't laugh out loud, but I saw glimmers of bemused smiles, a recognition of Jessica's wit and directness. There was a kind of murmur in the audience. That helped me. It gave me a moment to catch my breath, swallow, and release the tension in my throat. I also felt closer to my listeners, even though we were separated in the church by a vast space between us. I spoke more easily.

Being prepared with a story, particularly an amusing one, can help you and your listeners connect in a healing way. Also, a story or anecdote has a beginning, a middle, and an end that you can usually get through in spite of the emotions of the moment.

A note: This is one occasion at which I would advise you to write out your thoughts word for word, just in case you lose your place or are overcome with emotion.

Once you have made that initial connection, your conviction will empower your words. A eulogy may seem, at the outset, too daunting a task for you. My advice to you is, if you are asked or feel the need to offer your services, do not hesitate. I guarantee it will be an invaluable experience for you and your audience.

You, no doubt, face situations in the workplace or the community that you find challenging and, in some instances, scary. Whatever the special situation may be, the Seven Steps will guide you through it.

The First Aid Kit and the Emergency Kit

Be prepared.

THE MOTTO OF THE BOY SCOUTS OF AMERICA
AND THE GIRL SCOUTS OF AMERICA

This chapter is designed as a practical guide to help you handle emergency situations. The First Aid Kit deals with what to do when something goes wrong. You suddenly go blank, feel faint. You are thrown a curve and must speak off the cuff with *no* time to prepare. The First Aid Kit will see you through.

The Emergency Kit, on the other hand, deals with what to do when you have *very little* time to prepare. A few hours. Overnight. The stakes may be high. You cannot say no. There is no way out. Armed with your Emergency Kit, you no longer have to panic. You will know what to do.

The First Aid Kit

The First Aid Kit is intended for immediate relief.

Speaking off the Cuff

Talk about panic! There you are, minding your own business, getting ready to go into a meeting in which you expect to be left mercifully alone for a change, and the boss pulls you aside.

"Jennifer, you've got to help me out," he implores. "John is not going to be here for the introductions so you'll have to do them." Or picture this: What you thought was going to be a short symposium on your company's newest product line suddenly turns into a group discussion. The CEO turns to you and announces to everyone present, "Ralph was a key player on the team that developed our new line. Now, Ralph, what do you think would be our best strategy for launching it?"

Cultivate a way of thinking about projects with which you are involved that prepares you for the unexpected.

Go into each meeting, luncheon, or cocktail party you attend prepared to speak about what is uppermost on your mind that day. Set aside a half hour or so every week to review your immediate goals at work and the two or three points you want to make. Make sure you have framed your goals in a way that jibes with your higher objective. (This is what will ground you in conviction and give you strength.)

As projects progress and situations change, your goals may need to be revised slightly. Each morning, as you get ready for work, think this through: "If I am called upon today to explain what I'm doing, what will I say?" Practice the answer out loud until it comes easily. Use a tape recorder if necessary. As you prepare this way for off-the-cuff speaking, you'll be able to answer many of the questions you might be asked.

When you are thrown a curve, do not rush to answer right away. If you feel yourself panicking, take a deep breath. Hold onto an object: your memo pad, the edge of the desk, a pen. Plant your feet firmly on the floor. This will help get you grounded. Begin by making a human connection. You can acknowledge the question, rephrase it, or, in Ralph's case, you might say, "I'm flattered you are asking me for my input."

Don't try to be an authority if you're not. In the first scenario sketched out above, Jennifer doesn't have to give everyone present a definitive introduction. She could simply introduce each one by name and title and say something that sounds personal and appreciative.

Dialogue. Ask other people for additional input. If you know who really knows the nuts and bolts, refer your listeners to that authoritative source. Express a willingness to get back to the person who asked the question with additional information at a later time.

Creativity. When you are caught unprepared it's hard to be creative. However, the following exercise, practiced regularly, can help you to respond imaginatively and smoothly to the unexpected rather than freeze up and go blank.

Exercise for Speaking off the Cuff

You can do this exercise on your own or with a group of friends. Either way, you will need a stopwatch. If you do it on your own, choose a word at random out of a book, or close your eyes, open them, and choose as your subject the first object your gaze happens to light on. If you do it in a group, ask the group to throw you a topic.

Set the stopwatch for 60 seconds. Start it going without any time to prepare, and start talking. Here's an example of what one student did with the word *fish:*

> I love to eat fish, especially swordfish. Swordfish is absolutely delicious. Salmon is more fattening than swordfish. They both have fish oil. Fish oil is very, very good for you. It has something—I think it's called omega oil—in it and is recommended by many nutritionists. When I was a little girl I used to fish a lot in Michigan, and we used to catch blowfish in the lake, and we used to pop them by stamping on them with our feet. I also had goldfish. We used to buy them in little plastic bags. They had bright eyes and yellow flickering scales. And I had a goldfish tank, and they used to swim around through the seaweed and give me a lot of pleasure.

Sixty seconds.

Now you may be wondering what talking about fish has to do with speaking on the job. Your ability to think on your feet is like a muscle, and like a muscle, it can be developed. This exercise—which, incidentally, can be a lot of fun once you get going—will help develop your "muscle."

As a fearful speaker, you are accustomed to keeping a low profile, keeping your head down. In the past, that has meant going into meetings and trying to make yourself invisible. Now that you have worked through the Seven Step Program you can begin to think of "off the cuff" as another opportunity to speak, rather than as punishment.

Fielding Hostilities

You're sailing along, doing fine. Then suddenly, the CEO of one of your client corporations, who happens to be sitting in the front row, lets loose with this: "I'm sorry, but I think everything you've said so far is worthless." What do you do?

Ask for specifics. "Well, that's a possibility," you could reply, "but could you be more specific? What part of my analysis are you referring to?"

"The whole thing!" he replies belligerently.

"I'd be grateful for any suggestions you might have for improving it," you might parry. "Let's get together after the meeting. Meanwhile, however, I'd like to finish sketching out my game plan. It may help you change your mind."

If it is not the CEO of one of your client corporations who throws down the gauntlet, you do not need to suggest a meeting. "You are welcome to your opinion, but for a few more minutes I'll sketch out the rest of my game plan" is sufficient.

Asking for specifics helps defuse hostility. Do not engage in countering a hostile questioner's objections if his or her aggression is blatant. And remember, the audience will be on your side. If the person continues to interrupt, the audience will grow impatient and you can politely move on. Say something along the lines of, "I think you've made your point very clearly and everyone here has taken it in, but now I would like to move on and give everyone else here a chance to ask their questions as well."

When faced with a hostile assertion, the first thing you should do is ask for clarification. Rephrase the objection, using your own words, as in the following example.

Objection: "I'd never use your product, I think it's ineffective."

Your response: "You've had some bad experiences with our product? I'm sorry to hear that. Tell me a little bit about those experiences."

One word of caution: If you *know* they have a good point and can shoot holes in your product, admit the fault, take the ball back, and move on. For example: "Well, I'm sure everyone here is aware that last year we had some trouble with quality control but let me tell you about what we've done since then to improve things."

To sum up, when dealing with hostile questions:

- Take your time to focus.
- Ask for clarification unless you know you are opening a can of worms.

- After giving your questioner a chance to elaborate, acknowledge the person's point without necessarily supporting it, and move on.

Going Blank

If you prepare, you are less likely to go blank. But if you do go blank or lose your place, simply stop, take a deep breath, look down at your notes, and find your place. (This is one good reason always to bring notes along when you speak.) Search for your place and when you do get back on track, you don't need to point out that you were off of it. Nine times out of ten, the audience won't realize you're in trouble unless you announce it. Pausing can be a good thing. It gives your audience a chance to think about what you have said so far, to focus their attention. And if they do realize you have lost your place, remember: People are forgiving.

Dry Mouth

Have a glass of water with you. It is okay to pause and take a drink.

Shaky Hands

Hold onto something—the lectern, a small object. Remember: You may feel as though your hands are shaking badly, but it is usually not noticed by your audience. If you don't believe me, take a trusted friend with you the next time you make a presentation and ask if he or she could tell.

Handling Unexpected Disasters

Suppose you feel faint. Or your nose starts to bleed. Or you swallow the wrong way and are seized by an uncontrollable coughing fit. Relax! Tell or indicate to the audience that you need a moment. If you feel faint or start coughing, ask for a glass of water. If your nose starts to bleed, ask for some cotton and stop the bleeding. Then *move on*. Once again, remember: *You are only human*. If you don't *act* ashamed, you probably won't *be* ashamed, and you won't make your audience feel uncomfortable.

If you have seconds to prepare, call on two of the Seven Steps to get you through. They are:

1. Determine your objective. What can you do to make these off-the-cuff remarks worthwhile?

2. Think in terms of structure: a beginning, middle, and end.

Concentrate on these two steps. Keep concentrating on them until they materialize.

The Emergency Kit

It's 10 P.M. Instead of curling up under the covers with a good book, you are hurtling through the air on a nonstop flight to Montreal for a meeting tomorrow morning with key Canadian clients and a mission to "salvage the account."

It isn't your direct account. You aren't responsible for the mess in Montreal. You received your flying orders at six o'clock this evening, when your boss called you into his office to let you know—not ask you, but let you know—you were going. Just enough time to rush home, pack an overnight bag, grab a sheaf of notes fresh off the fax machine from your Montreal office, say a quick prayer to your patron saint, and hightail it to the airport.

Whenever you are asked to speak without sufficient time to prepare, the first thing to remember is that you are not the problem. The problem is the situation. The remedy is the Seven Steps.

If you try to cram three months' preparation into three hours, the odds are against you. Just isolate your objective and key points to achieve it. Focus on meanings, not a thousand facts. Try to arrange them into an intro, a body, and a conclusion.

Above all, do not waste time thinking about the time you don't have. Instead, use the time you do have. In the boarding area. On the plane. At the hotel. You have more time than you realize. At the prepanel cocktail party, slip into the ladies' room or men's room and go over your notes one last time.

Tools: A small notepad that's easy to scribble on can come in handy. If possible, bring a tape recorder along and use it to speak your thoughts out loud, as part of your practice time.

Go through the steps: Organize your thoughts. As you do so—structure the body of your presentation—double-check for persuasiveness. Are your arguments compelling? Decide how to get a response at the top. Plan your conclusion.

See if you can find a few more ways to engage in dialogue. (Don't worry about being creative. When you are under the gun, it's best to avoid an overreaching idea that you haven't had time to master.)

Use this presentation, as you will be using all your presentations, to give your audience the gift of your conviction—your belief in your company, its mission, its desire to give optimal service, whatever. Reread Step Seven and try to "connect to the core of what is meaningful to you," and speak from that place. Do this while planning your remarks and while delivering them.

One- to Six-Hour Preparation

I have listed in sequence the more important elements to prepare within a limited amount of time. If you have just one hour, follow this outline. If you have two hours, do the first and second hours of preparation, and so on.

First hour:

   Analyze the situation: audience, circumstance.

   Set an objective.

   Ideas for achieving the goal: explore possibilities, research.

Second hour:

   Set structure: Determine three main points and supporting points. For example:

   I. Main point
      A.
      B.
   II.
      A.
      B.
   III.
      A.
      B.

   Find response-getters to illustrate every point.

Third hour:

Talk into tape recorder. Practice your main argument or the body of your message out loud.

Establish content of:

Introduction

Body

Conclusion

Fourth hour:

Add your creative language and visuals.

Practice conclusion and introduction out loud.

Fifth hour:

Mark your outline.

Underline and circle key words.

Use slashes to clarify phrases.

Record—play back.

Clean up outline to make it legible.

Sixth hour:

Practice out loud.

Prepare answers for possible questions in Q&A.

Be a Fearless Speaker
Every Day

The problem that most people have at work is that they're always playing a role. . . . Once that happens, you become merely "pleasant." But "pleasant" isn't always very interesting. It doesn't give people a compelling reason to work on your projects or to be on your team. If you can engage people by expressing who you are, then they'll be excited to work with you.

BARBARA MOSES

By the time you get to this chapter, if you've been working on the program, you have already made at least six presentations! Whether you have done your public speaking in the context of a self-help workshop, in your place of work, in your community, or in front of a single empathetic friend, you have progressed toward becoming a fearless public speaker. You have stood up to your fears and said, "I won't let you rule my life!"

Now you must try to continue to challenge yourself! I urge you to make presentations as often as possible, because the best training is *experience*. Whenever the chance to speak in public comes up, seize it. And use your imagination to create additional opportunities.

Tom Pursues New Venues within His Career

Tom is a graphic artist. By the final session of class, he had made good progress.

"But what will I do now, Lilyan?" he said. "I meet with clients one on one all the time to sell my designs but I rarely have to speak in front of a group."

After talking about it, however, Tom realized he had used each one-on-one selling situation as an opportunity to apply the Seven Steps. He structured his remarks; he got a response at the top with a particular graphic, asked a direct question, or referred to something he admired about the prospective client's product line, and worked to keep a dialogue going. He made each presentation as creative as possible, bringing in a varied portfolio, or using mock-up designs, worked to be persuasive, clarified his objective, and tapped into his conviction.

After our talk, Tom contacted his alma mater, the Parsons School of Design, and offered to give a presentation to students on how to start their own businesses. The offer was accepted.

Then he contacted the Art Directors Club, of which he was a member, and reserved an evening to give a presentation showcasing his work. The presentation at Parsons was hugely rewarding for Tom, because it was an opportunity to give back to the community where he had first discovered his vocation. The presentation at the Art Directors Club led to six new accounts. The skills Tom used selling one on one proved to be very valuable in addressing the two groups. As a result, Tom more than doubled his client base. Meanwhile, his sense of himself as a fearless public speaker continued to grow.

Debbie Stays Active Even While out of Work

Another student, Debbie, came to my class after leaving a position at a major women's fashion magazine. "I'm taking this class because I want to improve my speaking skills," she said. "I'm honestly terrified every time I have to speak up in a staff meeting. And now I'm going to have to go back on the job interview circuit. Yuck!"

After completing the course, Debbie not only put together a mini-speech before each interview, she also volunteered her services to produce a fashion show sponsored by a resort hotel in upstate New York to benefit a philanthropic organization. The show featured three up-and-coming designers, and Debbie introduced each line herself. The show worked as an additional credit on her resume.

It was particularly impressive because it demonstrated initiative and creativity.

You, too, can find and/or initiate ways to practice and reinforce your new speaking skills. Begin by making a list of venues currently available to you.

Let's start with the workplace. Consider the following:

- Staff meetings
- Presentations in front of other departments
- Sales pitches before individual clients and client groups
- Training sessions

Are any of these part of your weekly/monthly routine? Could they be if you showed more initiative?

Every time you make *a presentation at work*—however short, however informal—see it as a chance to apply the Seven Step Program.

If you have to lead a meeting, plan to open with at least 30 seconds of introductory remarks. By planning to get a response at the top, by reaching out to engage your audience directly, by using a small creative touch, you can use even 30 seconds as an occasion to practice your skills.

Like Tom, when you *meet with clients* individually, think of yourself as giving a presentation. Do it when you have to make a presentation one on one to your boss. If you are the boss, or head a department, consider holding weekly staff meetings if you don't do so already.

Every time you *attend a group meeting*, take an active role. Don't fade into the woodwork. Come in with a prepared question, comment, or suggestion—one in keeping with your higher objective. Instead of sending a memo or e-mail to introduce a new idea, bring it up in a meeting. Or call a meeting to discuss it.

As your confidence grows, consider finding creative ways to use your new skills in fresh business-related arenas.

Across the country, networking groups have sprung up to help professionals meet one another and advertise their companies' services. Typically, such groups meet for a "power breakfast" and listen to a keynote speaker. Then each participant has one to three minutes to get up and *make a pitch* for what he or she does.

Consider joining such a group. They can be found in your local business journal—each week, *Crains* lists at least half a dozen networking groups meeting within the greater New York area. They are also frequently listed with your local chamber of commerce. Professional guilds, the local YMC/HA, and your college are other venues to consider. Call up and offer to speak about your area of expertise.

Get involved in your community. Jack, a junior litigator at a major New York law firm, came to me for help after a serious car accident left him very frightened and unsure about speaking in public. With my encouragement, he began to attend town meetings because he was concerned about local zoning changes. He soon became a passionate advocate of zoning control.

Pamela, who worked as a secretary in the foreign studies department of a small university, decided she cared deeply about the plight of Kurds in Iraq and called up local churches to volunteer her services to give informal talks about the subject.

Community involvement does not have to be about major public issues, however. Do you own a co-op? Is there something happening in the building that concerns you? Go to the next board meeting and talk about it. Co-op board meetings, PTA meetings, and community group meetings are all places where you can stand up and express your point of view.

Attend readings, symposia, and community events. When was the last time you went to an event of some kind and the speaker asked for questions or comments from the audience? Did you raise your hand? Next time, come prepared with an intelligent comment or question you'd like to explore.

Consider joining an organization or group where you will have opportunities to speak and can put the Seven Step Program to work. Here are a few suggestions for starters:

- *Book club*
- *Class* where you make presentations out loud
- *Civic or charitable organization*
- *Singles group/hobby club*
- *12-step program*
- *Toastmasters*

Look through your local paper or continuing education catalogs and target two or three programs that could interest you. Visit them. Choose one that feels right.

Consider teaching a class yourself. This may sound daunting, and it is not for everyone, but teaching can be one of the most empowering things you can do for yourself as a public speaker. Whether it's art or aerobics, mutual fund investment planning or meditation, we all have something we know something about. Suggest a course at your local community college: marketing strategies for small business owners, Japanese gardening, quilt making, how to write a good grant proposal. Less formally, you can offer a short workshop to a group of friends. Volunteer to lead a Sunday School class or to lead a discussion series at a neighborhood senior citizens' center.

Ask yourself: "Where can I make a contribution?" How can you apply your new skills as a fearless speaker to enrich the quality of your own life and the lives of those around you? Katherine, a freelance writer, was planning a big bash for her mother's 80th birthday. She planned to invite 65 guests. After taking my class, she decided that, not only would she provide music, food, wine, and hospitality, she would give a little speech about her mother—a verbal tribute. A year later, after her mother passed away, she looked back on this tribute as her greatest gift to the person she loved most in the world. Any time you go to a birthday, anniversary, wedding, shower, or tribute dinner, prepare in advance to make a toast or say something meaningful about the person being honored. It is one of the nicest things you can do. And if no one else is speaking up, then your remarks will be that much more meaningful.

There are countless other opportunities where you can share your life and experience of the world. You can give a talk at your child's school or at a community organization about a recent trip, your work, a community project with which you are involved.

Every time you go out—to a cocktail party, dinner, *or* special event—*prepare a topic for conversation.* It doesn't have to be something you've worked on for a week. After going through the Seven Steps, you can create a short conversation piece for such an occasion in 10 or 15 minutes. Refer to how Paul prepared his discourse on the joys of fine wines in Step Two. Think of a beginning, a middle, and an end; think of how you will get a response at the top; and so forth.

Each time you do this, you get another workout at delivering structured remarks. Every time, you take another small step forward.

Maintain Your Files

You should always be on the lookout for fresh quotes, interesting anecdotes, news stories, and op-eds related to your field. Develop a file of visual material as well. Jot down ideas for using props creatively as they occur to you. Collecting material will keep you on your toes, thinking of new ideas, new approaches for designing your presentations. And when your boss calls you up at the eleventh hour, telling you you're on a plane for Kalamazoo that very evening or you speak at a breakfast in Washington, D.C. the next week, you will have a reservoir of material to draw on.

Public speaking is an art. Like any art, it requires dedication and practice. If you have followed the Seven Step Program up to this point, you will have already tasted of the joys fearless speaking can bring: the magic of getting a response, the pleasure of tapping your own creativity, the power of persuasion, the overwhelming rightness one feels when speaking with an objective and from conviction.

But this is only a beginning. It is my fervent hope that *7 Steps to Fearless Speaking* becomes an ongoing resource for you, and that you continue to grow and to revel in your newfound voice.

> *Our deepest fear is not that we are inadequate. Our deepest fear is that we are powerful beyond measure. It is our light, not our darkness, that most frightens us. We ask ourselves, who am I to be brilliant, gorgeous, talented, fabulous? Actually, who are you not to be? You are a child of God. Your playing small doesn't serve the world. There's nothing enlightened about shrinking so that other people won't feel insecure around you. We were born to make manifest the glory of God that is within us. It's not just in some of us; it's in everyone. And as we let our own light shine, we unconsciously give other people permission to do the same."*

MARIANNE WILLIAMSON

▼

Voice Work

Voice Exercises

Here are your daily voice exercises. Start with Voice Exercise #1. Do that daily for one week. Then add an *additional* exercise each week in sequence until you are doing all seven every day (or as often as you can). You can devote as much time as you wish to practice but aim for at least 15 minutes each day. Doing all seven of the voice exercises will add up to about 30 to 45 minutes.

Enjoy the sound of your own voice!

Voice Exercise #1

LEARN TO RELAX

Slump back in your chair as if you were going to fall asleep. Let everything go. Let your arms hang at your sides, your legs stretch out in front of you, your head drop forward. Let your jaw relax. Feel all the tension drain out of your brow. Focus on tension, wherever you feel it. Say to yourself, silently, "Let go." If you feel like letting out some sound—a sigh or a laugh—do so. If you find yourself beginning to giggle, or if your eyes tear, or if you drool, don't worry. It means you are becoming more relaxed. Continue relaxing in this position for three to four minutes. Yawn. Open your throat. Let a deep "Ah" sound come out. Then sit up slowly. Open your eyes, and stand up slowly.

LEARN TO BREATHE PROPERLY

Place your hand on your midriff and inhale deeply. You will feel the diaphragm expand like a bellows. Exhale, and it contracts. You may inhale silently through your mouth. (You get more air that way.) Exhale through your nose. Do this exercise three times in a series of 10 breaths each.

AIROBICS FOR THE VOICE

1. *Projection*
   Focus on a spot far away.
   Try to get your voice to reach that spot.

2. *Support*
   Place one hand on your stomach and one hand on your diaphragm. Feel them expand, then pull your abdominal muscle *in* and your diaphragm *up,* saying:

   ONE!   w—UH—n   (one breath on each word)

   Do the same on each number, slowly, lingering on the vowels:

   TWO!   t—OO
   THREE!   thr—EE
   FOUR!   f—AW—r
   FIVE!   f—I—v

   Nothing but the abdomen and diaphragm should move. Shoulders and chest are steady.

3. *Vowels Extended*
   Now, count to five on one breath, lingering on the vowels, pulling the diaphragm and abdomen in slowly to use up all the space in your stomach, and to end:
   Repeat the count, continuing to breathe properly. Think of the vowels as a river with the sound flowing forward, and the consonants as the banks of the river containing the sound.

4. *Cheeks Up—Mouth Wide, Not Long, Only Open ¼ Inch*
   Keeping your cheek muscles up and your mouth widened in a slight smile automatically gives you better articulation. Also, it makes you look more alert.

5. *Pitch Low*
   A warm, mellow pitch is preferable to a high, nasal sound.
6. *Throat Open*
   Keeping your throat open, the back of your tongue down, and the soft palate raised, as they were when you were yawning, creates a resonating chamber for your voice.

Now, put it all together in this sequence of counts. Concentrate on all six techniques at the same time:

ONE through FIVE (on one breath), then double the tempo
ONE through TEN (on one breath), then triple the tempo
ONE through FIFTEEN (on one breath), then finally try to get all the numbers
ONE through TWENTY (on one breath)

Voice Exercise #2

SHIP! AHOY! HALT! FIRE! ALL ABOARD! HELP!
STAND BACK! BE GONE! WHO'S THERE? STAND HO!
AWAY, AWAY! BOUNCE!
CHARGE, CHESTER, CHARGE! ON, STANLEY, ON.
THE SEA, THE SEA, THE OPEN SEA!
WAKEN, LORDS AND LADIES GAY!
A HORSE! A HORSE! MY KINGDOM FOR A HORSE.
SAIL ON, SAIL ON, SAIL ON AND ON.
BOOMLAY, BOOMLAY, BOOMLAY, BOOM!

The words in this exercise should be said like the numbers exercise in Voice Exercise #1. Use the same six techniques, only instead of saying "*One* Two *Three*," say "SHIP! AHOY!" lingering on the vowel (sh-IH-IH-IH-p) (uh-h-AW-AW-AW-ih).

HALT   h-AW-AW-AW-lt
FIRE   f-AH-AH-AH-ir.

See if you can identify the vowels to linger on in the following words before checking the pronunciation below.

ALL ABOARD!

HELP!

STAND BACK!

BE GONE!

WHO'S THERE?

STAND HO!

AWAY, AWAY!

BOUNCE!

This is what these words should sound like with extended vowels:

ALL ABOARD!	(AW-AW-AW-l uh-BAW-AW-AW-rd)
HELP!	(h-EH-EH-EH-lp)
STAND BACK!	(st-AAA-AAA-nd b-AAA-AAA-ck)
BE GONE!	(b-EEE-EEE g-AW-AW-AW-n)
WHO'S THERE?	(wh-OOO-OOO-z th-AY-AY-AY-r)
STAND HO!	(st-AAA-AAA-nd h-OH-OH-OH)
AWAY, AWAY!	(uh-WAY-AY-AY, uh-WAY-AY-AY)
BOUNCE!	(b-AH-AH-AH-oons)

I'll underline the vowels to linger on for in the remainder of this exercise.

CHARGE, CHESTER, CHARGE! ON, STANLEY, ON!

THE SEA, THE SEA, THE OPEN SEA!

WAKEN, LORDS AND LADIES GAY!

A HORSE! A HORSE! MY KINGDOM FOR A HORSE!

SAIL ON, SAIL ON, SAIL ON AND ON!

BOOMLAY, BOOMLAY, BOOMLAY, BOOM!

Voice Exercise #3

Since vowels are like a river carrying the sound forward and consonants are like the banks of the river containing the sound, it is very important to be aware of their functions. Some consonants are pure air, while others are vibrated. In this exercise you learn to distinguish between unvoiced (pure air) consonants and voiced (vibrated) consonants.

The consonant P is not vibrated, it's unvoiced; while the consonant B, made in exactly the same position as P, is vibrated or voiced. Try not to let excessive air escape on P. In television that's called "popping your P's."

I call this exercise "The Waltz Exercise" because it is spoken with a waltz rhythm: ONE-two-three, ONE-two-three. The bold-faced **P** gets the strong sound; the light-faced P is virtually whispered. For the D sound, the tip of the tongue reaches up to the bony part of the palate. Straight and strong like an arrow, it hits the hard palate. Be sure to keep your cheek muscles up. This helps to articulate the consonants crisply. Continue with the K (unvoiced) and G (voiced). It is pronounced like this: *puh*, puh, puh, *buh*, buh, buh, etc.

PPP	**PPP**	**PPP**	**PAH,**	**PPP**	**PPP**	**PPP**	**PAY**
PPP	**PPP**	**PPP**	**PEE,**	**PPP**	**PPP**	**PPP**	**PAW**
PPP	**PPP**	**PPP**	**POH,**	**PPP**	**PPP**	**PPP**	**POO**
BBB	**BBB**	**BBB**	**BAH,**	**BBB**	**BBB**	**BBB**	**BAY**
BBB	**BBB**	**BBB**	**BEE,**	**BBB**	**BBB**	**BBB**	**BAW**
BBB	**BBB**	**BBB**	**BOH,**	**BBB**	**BBB**	**BBB**	**BOO**
DDD	**DDD**	**DDD**	**DAH,**	**DDD**	**DDD**	**DDD**	**DAY**
DDD	**DDD**	**DDD**	**DEE,**	**DDD**	**DDD**	**DDD**	**DAW**
DDD	**DDD**	**DDD**	**DOH,**	**DDD**	**DDD**	**DDD**	**DOO**
KKK	**KKK**	**KKK**	**KAH,**	**KKK**	**KKK**	**KKK**	**KAY**
KKK	**KKK**	**KKK**	**KEE,**	**KKK**	**KKK**	**KKK**	**KAW**
KKK	**KKK**	**KKK**	**KOH,**	**KKK**	**KKK**	**KKK**	**KOO**
GGG	**GGG**	**GGG**	**GAH,**	**GGG**	**GGG**	**GGG**	**GAY**
GGG	**GGG**	**GGG**	**GEE,**	**GGG**	**GGG**	**GGG**	**GAW**
GGG	**GGG**	**GGG**	**GOH,**	**GGG**	**GGG**	**GGG**	**GOO**

Voice Exercise #4

This exercise prepares you for *emphasis*. While you are delivering a speech, it is important to determine what the key words and phrases are. I use the following exercise to warm up the muscles of expression. It should be done in an exaggerated way, using the extremes of your sound to make certain syllables heavy and certain syllables light. In your mind, as you say them, you think, "*Heavy*, light, light, light, *heavy*, light, light, light." I've underlined the heavy syllables. Syllables that are not underlined are light. Every time you say a heavy syllable, your diaphragm and abdomen contract (as they do when you do the numbers, commands, and waltz exercises).

After you've practiced this many, many times (maybe 100), you will automatically contract your diaphragm and abdomen. It's hard to predict when you will be able to carry this over to your everyday speaking. It depends on how much and how well you practice.

Extend one hand over your diaphragm and your abdomen. Hold this exercise sheet in the other. Stand. Project to a spot far away. Expand your diaphragm and abdomen. Contract them on the underlined syllables.

> <u>RATS</u>!
> THEY <u>FOUGHT</u> THE DOGS, AND <u>KILLED</u> THE CATS
> AND <u>BIT</u> THE BABIES <u>IN</u> THE CRADLES,
> AND <u>ATE</u> THE CHEESES <u>OUT</u> OF THE VATS,
> AND <u>LICKED</u> THE SOUP FROM THE <u>COOKS'</u> OWN LADLES,
> SPLIT <u>OP</u>EN THE KEGS OF <u>SAL</u>TED SPRATS,
> MADE <u>NESTS</u> INSIDE MEN'S <u>SUN</u>DAY HATS,
> AND <u>EV</u>EN SPOILED THE <u>WO</u>MEN'S CHATS,
>   BY <u>DROWN</u>ING THEIR SPEAKING
>   WITH <u>SHRIE</u>KING AND SQUEAKING
> IN <u>FIF</u>TY DIFFERENT <u>SHARPS</u> AND FLATS.

Do this again. Keep thinking, "*Heavy*, light, light, light." Audiotape it the second time. Listen. Is it as heavy and as light as you can make it? Practically whisper the light words. Now on to the second part.

Put one hand on your diaphragm and your abdomen. Hold this exercise sheet in the other. Stand. Project to a spot far away. Expand your diaphragm and abdomen. Contract them on the underlined syllables.

> GREAT RATS, SMALL RATS, LEAN RATS, BRAWNY RATS,
> BROWN RATS, BLACK RATS, GREY RATS, TAWNY RATS,
> GRAVE OLD PLODDERS, GAY YOUNG FRISKERS,
>   FATHERS, MOTHERS, UNCLES, COUSINS,
> COCKING TAILS AND PRICKING WHISKERS,
>   FAMILIES BY TENS AND DOZENS,
> BROTHERS, SISTERS, HUSBANDS, WIVES—
> FOLLOWED THE PIPER FOR THEIR LIVES.

Voice Exercise #5

Articulation should be seamless, unnoticeable. In other words, we articulate to make clear what we're saying, not to make consonants and vowels stand out for their own sake.

This selection from Gilbert and Sullivan's *Iolanthe* is fun to say and excellent for shaping articulation muscles—the tip of the tongue against the hard palate, the thrust of the tongue, the cheek muscles, the lips. It's also good for practicing rhythm. Try to take a quick, short breath at the end of each line, regardless of whether you need it, so that you realize you don't have to talk, talk, talk, until you run out of breath. Take a breath *before* you run out of it.

I've underlined the syllables you should hit a little harder than the rest.

"LORD CHANCELLOR'S SONG," *IOLANTHE* ACT II

When you're lying awake with a dismal headache, and your repose
    is taboo'd by anxiety,
I conceive you may use any language you choose to indulge in,
    without impropriety;
For your brain is on fire—the bedclothes conspire of usual slumber
    to plunder you:
First your counterpane goes, and uncovers your toes, and your
    sheet slips demurely from under you;
Then the blanketing tickles—you feel like mixed pickles—so terri-
    bly sharp is the pricking,

And you're <u>hot</u>, and you're cross, and you <u>tum</u>ble and toss till there's <u>noth</u>ing 'twixt you and the <u>tick</u>ing.

Then the <u>bed</u>clothes all creep to the <u>ground</u> in a heap, and you <u>pick</u> 'em all up in a <u>tan</u>gle;

Next your <u>pil</u>low resigns and po<u>lite</u>ly declines to re<u>main</u> at its usual <u>an</u>gle!

If you have more time and want to do the entire piece, do so. If not, stick with the first paragraph and repeat it two or three times, making the consonants crisp and lingering on the vowels of the words underlined.

Well, you <u>get</u> some repose in the <u>form</u> of a doze, with hot <u>eye</u>balls and head ever <u>ach</u>ing.

But your <u>slum</u>bering teems with such <u>hor</u>rible dreams that you'd <u>ve</u>ry much better be <u>wak</u>ing;

For you <u>dream</u> you are crossing the <u>Chan</u>nel, and tossing a<u>bout</u> in a steamer from <u>Har</u>wich—

Which is <u>some</u>thing between a large <u>bath</u>ing machine and a <u>ve</u>ry small second-class <u>car</u>riage—

And <u>bound</u> on that journey you <u>find</u> your attorney (who <u>start</u>ed that morning from <u>Dev</u>on);

He's a <u>bit</u> undersized, and you <u>don't</u> feel surprised when he <u>tells</u> you he's only el<u>ev</u>en.

Well, you're <u>driv</u>ing like mad with this <u>sin</u>gular lad (by the <u>by</u>, the ship's now a four-<u>wheel</u>er),

And you're <u>play</u>ing round games, and he <u>calls</u> you bad names when you <u>tell</u> him that "ties pay the <u>deal</u>er";

But <u>this</u> you can't stand, so you <u>throw</u> up your hand, and you <u>find</u> you're as cold as an <u>i</u>cicle,

In your <u>shirt</u> and your socks (the black <u>silk</u> with gold clocks), cross-ing <u>Sal</u>isbury Plain on a <u>bi</u>cycle:

And <u>he</u> and the crew are on <u>bi</u>cycles too—which they've <u>some</u>how or other in<u>vest</u>ed in—

And he's <u>tell</u>ing the tars all the <u>par</u>ticulars of a <u>com</u>pany he's inter<u>est</u>ed in—

The <u>shares</u> are a penny, and <u>e</u>ver so many are <u>ta</u>ken by Rothschild and <u>Ba</u>ring,
And <u>just</u> as few are al<u>lot</u>ted to you, you a<u>wake</u> with a shudder despairing—<u>(accelerate pace)</u>
You're a <u>re</u>gular wreck, with a <u>crick</u> in your neck, and no <u>won</u>der you snore, for your <u>head's</u> on the floor, and you've <u>need</u>les and pins from your <u>soles</u> to your shins, and your <u>flesh</u> is a-creep, for your <u>left</u> leg's asleep, and you've a <u>cramp</u> in your toes, and a <u>fly</u> on your nose, and some <u>fluff</u> in your lung, and a <u>fe</u>verish tongue, and a <u>thirst</u> that's intense, and a <u>ge</u>neral sense that you <u>ha</u>ven't been sleeping in <u>cl</u>over;
But the <u>dark</u>ness has passed, and it's <u>day</u>light at last, <u>(slow down)</u>
And the <u>night</u> has been long—ditto <u>dit</u>to my song—
And thank <u>good</u>ness they're both of them <u>o</u>ver!

This is a long piece. Do it in sections where I've left spaces. (One day do the first section, another day the second section, and a third day the last.) Have fun with it. (Be sure to verbalize Z and J sounds.)

Voice Exercise #6

Our voices are made up of many musical components: melody, rhythm, pitches, beats, crescendos, pianissimos, and fortes.

The poem "The Highwayman," by Alfred Noyes, is one that lends itself to practicing all the nuances of music. It also invites you to use onomatopoeia. For instance, in the first sentence, try to make the words sound like what they say: "The wind was a torrent of darkness among the gusty trees." Try to make the word "wind" sound like the wind; "torrent of darkness" like an ominous torrent or dark rain; "the gusty trees" like the whipping and swishing of leaves and branches in a fierce storm. Try to have your voice paint the picture.

"The moon was a ghostly galleon"—make it very still and mysterious. "Tossed upon cloudy seas"—here's an active image of the ocean's waves, colored by "cloudy." Let your imagination soar and your voice will reflect it.

"The road was a ribbon of moonlight"—use the alliteration of the "r" sound, which carries over into the repetition of the word "riding" to do another kind of musical riff, and make the word "moonlight" sound like an image of the moon.

When you get to "And the highwayman came riding—riding, riding—the highwayman came riding, up to the old inn door": Begin the first "riding" in a low pitch, quietly, and gradually work up to the fourth "riding" in intensity and rising pitch. Make the fourth "riding" the strongest and most full in tone.

This is a wonderful poem to explore for variety of sound, musicality, and dynamics of voice. Have a good time with it. There's no right way—or wrong way. This is your experimenting, reading, and enjoying time.

THE HIGHWAYMAN

Part I

The wind was a torrent of darkness among the gusty trees,
The moon was a ghostly galleon tossed upon cloudy seas.
The road was a ribbon of moonlight over the purple moor,
And the highwayman came riding—
Riding—riding—
The highwayman came riding, up to the old inn-door.

He'd a French cocked-hat on his forehead, a bunch of lace at his chin,
A coat of the claret velvet, and breeches of brown doe-skin.
They fitted with never a wrinkle. His boots were up to the thigh.
And he rode with a jeweled twinkle,
His pistol butts a-twinkle,
His rapier hilts a-twinkle, under the jeweled sky.

Over the cobbles he clattered and clashed in the dark inn-yard.
He tapped with his whip on the shutters, but all was locked and barred.
He whistled a tune to the window, and who should be waiting there
But the landlord's black-eyed daughter,
Bess, the landlord's daughter,
Plaiting a dark red love-knot into her long black hair.

There are several more verses to the poem. Look it up, if you want to know how the story ends.

Voice Exercise #7

Shakespeare offers endless, valuable, and beautiful verbal material with which to practice—from *Romeo and Juliet* to *King Lear*, from *Twelfth Night* to *Julius Caesar*. One of my favorite passages provides variety of pitch, rhythm, and volume. It is Marullus's speech from *Julius Caesar* to the crowd. Imagine that you are trying to quiet the noisy rabble. Top them with your energy and sound as you say: "Wherefore rejoice? . . ." through "Knew you not Pompey?"

Now say quickly, on one breath: "Many a time and oft have you climb'd up to walls and battlements, to towers and windows, yea, to chimney-tops . . ." Take another breath and speak quickly and clearly: "Your infant in your arms, and there have sat the live-long day with patient expectation to see great Pompey pass the streets of Rome." Slow down and say each sentence in two parts: "And when you saw . . . his chariot but appear . . . Have you not made . . . an universal shout." Make the word "shout" go up in pitch; "Made in her concave shores," very low in pitch. Then in a sarcastic way, "And do you now put on your best attire? And do you now cull out a holiday? And do you now strew flower in his way that comes in triumph over Pompey's blood." Hit the word "blood," and even stronger "Be gone!" Build in interest and pitch each of the next images, "Run to your houses, fall upon your knees." Say the last line on one breath very strongly, "Pray to the gods to intermit the plague that needs must light on this ingratitude."

> **Wherefore rejoice? What conquest brings he home?**
> **What tributaries follow him to Rome,**
> **To grace in captive bonds his chariot-wheels?**
> **You blocks, you stones, you worse than senseless things!**
> **O you hard hearts, you cruel men of Rome,**
> **[Breathe]**
> **Knew you not Pompey? Many a time and oft**
> **Have you climb'd up to walls and battlements,**
> **To towers and windows, yea, to chimney-tops, [Breathe]**

Your infants in your arms, and there have sat
The live-long day with patient expectation
To see great Pompey pass the streets of Rome: [Breathe]
And when you saw his chariot but appear,
Have you not made an universal shout,
That Tiber trembled underneath her banks
To hear the replication of your sounds
Made in her concave shores?
And do you now put on your best attire?
And do you now cull out a holiday?
And do you now strew flowers in his way
That comes in triumph over Pompey's blood?
Be gone!
Run to your houses, fall upon your knees,
Pray to the gods to intermit the plague
That needs must light on this ingratitude.

This passage is a good workout to do each day. Do the other exercises each day as well. Use whatever works for you. There's a world of literature to choose from. By this time, you could easily be taking 30 minutes each day to relax, breathe, and vocalize the exercises of the Seven Steps. Get in the habit of hearing your voice, developing your sound, and enjoying what you hear.

Caring for Your Voice

Your voice is a musical instrument. And like an instrument, it must be treated with care. A musician knows that a piano, violin, or clarinet must be in top condition in order to get the best sound out of it. The voice is in that category, as well.

What distinguishes the human voice, however, is that it is part of the human body. There is a direct connection between the voice and the body. When your body is tired or sick, it is reflected in your voice. Your voice loses its elasticity and flexibility. The tone is affected. Articulation is limp. Your breathing comes in short spurts. If you have learned how to relax, breathe, and practice voice exercises regularly, your voice will suffer less when you are tired or ill. Like any muscle in your body, the vocal cords get stronger through practice and proper use.

It's important to remember that the trachea is used for two purposes: It is the tube that houses your vocal cords, and it is the tube through which your food passes to be digested. That is why you cannot speak and swallow foods or liquids at the same time, why you sometimes choke or have a coughing spell while speaking. You may just be swallowing saliva and you start coughing. The apparatus of the voice and the larynx and the part of the body that houses the larynx are closely involved in making sound.

Your mind determines what you're saying and dictates what words you use. It is the second important element in caring for your voice. If you are muddled in your thinking, tired, or not sure of what you're saying, your voice will reflect that. So in addition to keeping your voice healthy, it is important to know what you want to say, and say it in a manner that reflects your thinking.

To keep your voice strong and in good shape physically, it is important that your body be relaxed. That is why you may note that after lovemaking your voice is richer sounding. Lower notes, more musical tones, and calmer rhythm comes through. This leads to the third element of healthy sound, the soul.

When you are in love, content in a relationship, or at one with yourself, your voice is more mellow. It just is. You can determine whether your sound will be musical, vibrant, beautiful, and engulfing—just as you determine when to relax, meditate, and/or pray. Your voice is the mirror of your soul.

Keeping your voice healthy is a result of body, mind, and soul working in concert with you.

Try to set up a daily routine of exercises. Start with the series put together in this book. If you have the time and inclination, you can practice as much as an hour each day for relaxation, breathing, and voice exercises. If you cannot or don't want to do that, at least do the basics. Exercises 1, 2, 3, and 4 should take about 15 to 20 minutes. Then during the day, if you have occasion to read aloud to your children (before bedtime), or if you join a chorus or choir and sing, or if you just make the effort to sound better, it will all add up to a better and more reliable voice.

In addition, here are practical tips to follow to keep your voice healthy:

- Keep your voice in good physical condition by practicing daily.
- Enjoy hearing your sound. Remember, you determine it.
- When getting up to speak before a group, always have a glass of water handy. Even at a eulogy (as I did when I gave Jessica Savitch's eulogy), guarding against a possible choking or tightening of the vocal cords is important.
- Before speaking, do not eat dairy products—milk, butter, cream, soft cheese. (They coat the vocal cords.) Avoid nuts. (They irritate the trachea.) Do not drink liquor or wine before speaking. Liquor increases mucus in the throat. It also affects your ability to think.
- Get proper rest.
- Don't abuse your vocal cords by shouting, screaming, or trying to be heard in a noisy place.
- Polish your instrument (particularly when you're ill) with warm tea (not too hot or not too cold) with honey and lemon.
- Use lozenges that keep your throat moist.
- Don't smoke. With each inhalation your throat becomes inflamed. It takes 15 minutes for your throat to get back to normal to restore itself from the damage done by the heat of the cigarette.

13 Commonly Mispronounced Words

Correct Spelling	Wrong Pronunciation	Right Pronunciation
ACTS	AKS	AKTS
ASKED	AKS	ASKT
ETCETERA	EK SET ER UH	ET SÉT ER UH
FACTS	FAKS	FAKTS

Correct Spelling	Wrong Pronunciation	Right Pronunciation
FIFTH	FITH or FIF	FÍFTH
GENUINE	JEN YU WINE	JEN YU IN
HUNDRED	HUN DERT	HÚN DRED
INTERNATIONAL	INNERNASHUNAL	IN TER NÁ SHUH NAL
INTRODUCE	INNERDOOS	IN TRO DYÓOS
NUCLEAR	NOOKYOULUHR	NÓO KLEE UHR
PICTURE	PI CHUR	PÍK CHUR
PRODUCTS	PRAH DUKS	PRAH DUKTS
RECOGNIZED	REKUNIZED	RE KUG NIZD

Note: Practice "ACTS" and "FACTS" as if they are two-syllable words, e.g., AK-TS and FAK-TS, otherwise you might eliminate that all important "T". The "T" and the "S" are pronounced as one sound, but the "T" must be there. Otherwise, "ACTS" becomes "AX" and "FACTS" becomes "FAX."

▼

If You Need Medical Help

I know from long experience that this Seven Step Program works. However, it's possible that your fear of speaking is rooted in a childhood trauma or another medical condition that is so deep-seated that additional help is necessary.

Several of my students receive additional counseling or medical treatment while they are studying the Seven Step Program. Some are receiving medication. A family of drugs called beta-blockers has proven helpful to some. Beta-blockers reduce the physical symptoms of fear by reducing blood pressure and slowing the heartbeat.

Do you need medication to overcome your fear of speaking? That's a question I can't answer here. But if you think you may need help beyond what this program offers, please do not delay in seeking it.

If you think you need additional help and aren't sure where to go, here are some suggestions:

- The Anxiety Disorders Association of America, a national, nonprofit partnership of consumers, researchers, and health care practitioners. Write to the ADAA at 11900 Parklawn Dr., Suite 100, Rockville, MD 20852. Call 301-231-9350. E-mail: Anxdis@aol.com. Web site: www.adaa.org.

- Hollins Communications Research Institute (for problems with stuttering), P.O. Box 9737, Roanoke, VA 24020 (mailing address); located at 7851 Enon Drive, Roanoke, VA 24019. Call 540-265-5650. E-mail: adm-hcri@rbnet.com. Web site: www.stuttering.org.

- Jerilyn Ross, M.A., L.I.C.S.W., The Ross Center for Anxiety and Related Disorders, 4545 42nd St., NW, Suite 311, Washington, DC 20016. Call 800-545-7367 or 202-363-1010. E-mail: Jerilyn@rosscenter.com. Web site: www.rosscenter.com.
- Donald F. Klein, M.D., New York Psychiatric Institute, Columbia Presbyterian Hospital, 1051 Riverside Dr., New York, NY 10032. Call 212 543-2366.
- Michael R. Leibowitz, M.D., New York Psychiatric Institute, Columbia Presbyterian Hospital, 1051 Riverside Dr., New York, NY 10032. Call 212-543-5366.

Call your local community mental health referral service. Many major teaching hospitals also have clinics and other special programs for treatment of anxiety disorders.

These are eight of my favorite selections to read aloud. Seek them out and try reading them aloud yourself. I feel it is important in addition to doing the daily voice exercises, that you hear your own voice stretching to express sounds you may not have ever made before. Also, sharing the wonderful world of literature with others—be it your friends, children, or colleagues—is a joyful and exhilarating experience.

1. "The Cataract of Lodore"—poem by Robert Southey. Concentrate on onomatopoeia.

2. *The Old Man and the Sea*—novel by Ernest Hemingway. Note the sensual language, and the rich, short sentences.

3. Sonnets by William Shakespeare. Listen to the music of the words and connect to the sentiment.

4. "Do Not Go Gentle into That Good Night"—poem by Dylan Thomas. Explore the passion and the pain.

5. *The Odd Couple*—play by Neil Simon. Oscar tells Felix exactly what it is Felix does that bugs him. His exasperation and recounting of details are very funny.

6. "Still I Rise"—poem by Maya Angelou. The historic, daring drama of Maya Angelou's view of slavery.

7. *A Streetcar Named Desire*—play by Tennessee Williams. Blanche describes to her sister Stella how she suffered as the members of the family died, and why she is left penniless after paying medical and funeral expenses.

8. "Lament"—poem by Dylan Thomas. Listen to the sounds of the words, not necessarily the meaning.

ACKNOWLEDGMENTS

▼

I am grateful to the following people for helping me put this book together:

Priscilla Shanks, my associate, for her constancy, her thorough understanding of our teaching process and her joy in the work.

Katherine Kormendi for being there at its inception years ago. For her keen thinking, her inventive ideas and her vision.

James Baker, my assistant, for his logic and never-tiring attention to a myriad of details, plus his good cheer and resourcefulness.

Edward Hayman, for having the ability to put my eyes and ears, my values and teaching method into words—and for doing it with style.

Frances C. Jones, for her editing skills, good taste, and up-to-the-minute awareness of the book publishing business, plus always being there for me.

Steve Zousmer, for his incisive, witty, honest, erudite reading of the manuscript.

Joyce Engelson who, through the years and all the versions of the manuscript, encouraged me to believe that this is a worthwhile and needed book.

Alayne Courtney, whose buoyant spirit and historic and worldly knowledge gave the book more depth.

Cora Lee Five, writer and teacher, who guided me through the teaching process on the page with logic and spirit.

Jean Carper who was always available to talk me through difficult, trying moments and to add her successful experience as a writer to the logic of the process.

Alanna Nash, ever faithful friend, knowledgeable and encouraging, with class.

Elizabeth Esch, whose nighttime calls provided a healthy dose of reality, and made me laugh.

Eva Rosenstein, whose practical thinking brought me comfort during numerous midnight calls.

Ruth Mills, my editor at John Wiley & Sons, for her guidance and steadfast spirit.

Barbara Lowenstein, my agent.

My students, past, present, and future, who bring my work to fruition.

INDEX